Rushing Ahead to Armageddon

Russia, Iran and the Invasion of Israel

Christopher M Jones

XUION
PRESS

—⟋⟍—

To my wife Michelle who constantly encouraged me while writing my first book. To my parents Irv and Connie for the godly foundation that they gave me as a child and without their help this book would not have been published and my sister Erica who gave me great feedback on this book.

Table of Contents

—⟋⟍—

CHAPTER ONE

Rushing Ahead to Armageddon

—⟋⟋⟍—

"The end of the world as we know it is rapidly approaching"[1]

- John Hagee

In January 2006, popular prophecy teacher John Hagee, founder and senior pastor of Cornerstone Church in San Antonio, Texas, released a book titled *Jerusalem Countdown: A Warning to the World*. In its initial release in January 2006, it sold over 627, 0000 copies. It made number one on Wal-Mart's inspirational titles list, it was on USA Today's Top 50 best selling books for nine weeks, and was number two in the Publisher Weekly April 2006 Bestseller's list[2]. Due to its overwhelming success, pastor Hagee published a revised and updated version of *Jerusalem Countdown* exactly one year later pushing sales of the book to over one million copies sold. Both versions were heralding an impending nuclear crisis that is centered on Iran and Israel that could possibly push the world closer to Armageddon. At a July 19, 2006 CUFI event in Washington D.C., Hagee told the audience, "The United States must join Israel in a pre-emptive military strike against Iran to fulfill God's plan for both Israel and the West ... a biblically prophesied end-time confrontation with Iran, which will lead to the Rapture, Tribulation [...] and [the] Second Coming of Christ."[3]

According to Pastor Hagee, "We are on a countdown to crisis. A nuclear showdown with Iran is apparent. The battle for Jerusalem has begun. This war will affect every person on planet earth."[4] His revised and updated version states that "World War III has begun! There will soon be a nuclear blast in the Middle East that will transform the road to Armageddon into a racetrack. America and Israel will either take down Iran, or Iran will become nuclear and attempt to take down America and Israel."[5] He believes that "unless the entire world-including America, Israel, and the

Middle East-reaches a soon diplomatic and peaceful resolution to Iran's nuclear threat, Israel and America will be on a nuclear collision course with Iran."[6] Hagee is staunchly pro-Israel and is the founder and national chairman of Christians United for Israel. In his many writings, he sees historical and contemporary events, especially in the Middle East, as unfolding biblical prophecy.[7] Pastor Hagee "is convinced recent armed conflict in the Middle East and the specter of Iran are proof that the apocalyptic battle of Armageddon - the war to end all wars to be fought in Israel - is not far off."[8] Hagee believes that "Iran will lead a coalition of Islamic countries, also supported by Russia, in a nuclear attack on Israel. The event Hagee says will kick-off the real mother of all battles – Armageddon, the final great earthly war first mentioned in the Book of Revelation. According to Hagee, this war between "Islamo-fascists" and the Christians and Jews has already begun and will over its course consume countless Israeli lives."[9]

Before *Jerusalem Countdown* was even published Pastor Hagee maintained, "The coming nuclear showdown with Iran is a certainty. The war of Ezekiel 38-39 could begin before this book gets published."[10] Although no war has broken out against Iran since the release of both versions of his book, with all of the news that is coming from Iran and Russia there is a chance that he could very well be correct.

Iran: A State Sponsor of Terror

The nation of Iran, ever since the Islamic revolution that sent the Shah into exile in 1979, has been a country that has been dedicated to terror. Shahram Chubin, Director of Studies at the Geneva Centre for Security Policy, and an expert on Iran's foreign and security policies, examined the evolving uses of terror by the Iranian regime during the Islamic Republic's history. Chubin noted that the Iranian regime is a revolutionary one, which has "used terror to sustain its power." Its main goal has been to export the revolution to other parts of the region, with the aim of forcefully driving other powers out of the region (mainly Israel and the United States), and as a "continuing need to bolster domestic legitimacy." He emphasized that terrorism has not only been an important instrument in exporting the revolution, but has been done at a very low cost and low risk to Iran, and has proven effective.[11] In order to export its revolution, Iran has reached out to terror organizations that agree with its ideals.

Tehran openly provides funding, training, and weapons to the world"s worst terrorists, including Hezbollah, Hamas, the Palestinian Islamic Jihad, and the Popular Front for the Liberation of Palestine, and it has a cozy relationship with al Qaeda. It has given sanctuary to major al Qaeda terrorists, including senior military commander Saif al-Adel, three of Osama bin Laden's sons, and al Qaeda spokesman Suleiman Abu Ghaith. It supports many of the barbaric terrorists in Iraq who are murdering innocent civilians in order to destroy Iraq's fragile hold on democracy.[12] The one terror organization that has been the biggest benefactor of Iranian support has been Hezbollah.

Iran and Hezbollah

"Hezbollah (translated as "Party of God") traces its roots to Najaf in Iraq. Najaf is an important Shi'ite center of theology with an important position in Islamic history. Here [in Najaf] is buried the Imam Ali, whom Shi'ites Muslims consider the first convert of Mohammad and the rightful successor to the Prophet. Ayatollah Muhammad Hussein Fadlallah, the spiritual leader of Hezbollah, studied in Najaf when he was in exile from Lebanon; there he met and studied under Ayatollah Khomeini, who himself was in exile from Iran. Hezbollah as an organization arose in 1982 from the disorder in the Lebanese Shi'ite community caused by civil war. Since its inception, Hezbollah has embraced terrorism as its principal methodology to achieve its major jihadist goals: (1) to conduct a relentless struggle against the State of Israel with a view to "liberate" Jerusalem and annihilate the Jewish state, and (2) to force the United States out of the Middle East as the first step in defeating America worldwide. From the beginning, Hezbollah has held out the dream of a worldwide conquest of Shi'ite ideology, with the aim of establishing the hegemony of a Shi'ite theocracy around the globe."[13]

Even though Iran is hundreds of miles away from Lebanon, it has helped nurture Hezbollah in its early years and even today exercises considerable ideological and operational influence.[14] "With Iranian guidance, the Lebanese Hezbollah dramatically captured America's attention with devastating suicide attacks on the U.S. Embassy in Beirut in April 1983, where 63 people died, including 17 Americans, and on the U.S. Marine Barracks in October 1983, where 241 U.S. Marines were killed (a simultaneous attack killed 58 French peacekeepers). These attacks, and the sense that the peacekeepers had little peace to keep, led President Reagan to withdraw U.S. troops in February 1984. Hezbollah also took numerous Westerners hostage in the 1980's executing several of them. Hezbollah after working through suborganizations with different names, took 17 Americans, 15 Frenchmen, 14 Britons, 7 Swiss, and 7 West Germans hostage, as well as 17 others hostage during the 1980's. In March 1992, Hezbollah and Iran worked together to bomb the Israeli Embassy in Argentina, killing 29 and in July 1994 attacked the Jewish Community Center in Buenos Aires, killing 86."[15]

After the 1982-2000 guerrilla conflict against Israel, that many believed was instigated by Iran, Hezbollah seemed to disappear from the news headlines. In July of 2006, they roared back into the headlines in a 34-day conflict with Israel. The conflict started when Hezbollah operatives, at the instigation of what many believe was Iran, kidnapped Israeli soldiers who were patrolling the Israeli side of the border in northern Israel and was ended by a United Nations brokered ceasefire on August 14, 2006.

It appears now that Hezbollah is also getting involved in Iraq. "U.S. forces for the first time accused Hezbollah of playing a direct role in the violence plaguing Iraq, as America hardened its rhetoric against the group's backers in Iran. Brigadier General Kevin Bergner, a US military spokesman in Baghdad, accused Hezbollah, a Lebanese Shia group which is funded and trained by Iran, of fomenting violence in Iraq along with an overseas wing of Iran's Revolutionary Guards."[16]

"Brig. Gen. Bergner said Iraqi extremists were taken to Iran in groups of 20 to 60 for training in three camps "not too far from Tehran." When the militants returned to Iraq, they formed units called "special groups" to carry out attacks, bombings and kidnappings. The Quds force and Hezbollah were jointly operating camps near Tehran in which they trained Iraqi fighters before sending them back to Iraq to wage attacks, the US military spokesman said."[17]

In late 2007, four Hezbollah operatives who were captured in Iraq admitted to receiving their training in Iran. According to the captured operatives the training "is carried out at several camps near Tehran that are overseen by the Quds Force of the Islamic Revolutionary Guard Command, and the instruction is carried out by militants from Hezbollah, which has long been supported by the Quds Force."[18] According to a *New York Times* report, "The militants then return to Iraq to teach other militants how to fire rockets and mortars, fight as snipers or assemble explosively formed penetrators, a particularly lethal type of roadside bomb made of Iranian components, according to American officials. The officials describe this approach as "training the trainers.""[19]

Jerome Corsi reported in his book *Atomic Iran* how "Western intelligence sources estimate that Hezbollah operates on an annual budget of approximately one hundred million dollars, most of which comes from Iran. These funds go toward funding terrorist activities as well as paying for the operation of Hezbollah communal organizations such as schools and hospitals. On its own, Hezbollah probably raises another fifty million dollars per year over and above the one hundred million dollars provided by Iran. Hezbollah raises considerable funds through Islamic "charities" worldwide, front organizations that appear to serve legitimate community needs but whose real purpose is to act as subterfuge for funneling money to Hezbollah terrorists. Hezbollah also engages in the typical activities of an organized crime syndicate: trafficking in illegal drugs and money counterfeiting (especially U.S. one-hundred-dollar bills). Other forms of criminal activity include cigarette smuggling, car thefts, and credit card forgery."[20]

Iran and Hamas

Hamas (in Arabic, an acronym for "Harakat Al-Muqawama Al-Islamia" — Islamic Resistance Movement — and a word meaning courage and bravery) is a radical Islamic fundamentalist organization which became active in the early stages of the intifada, operating primarily in the Gaza District but also in Judea and Samaria. Hamas is the strongest opposition group to the peace process, to the PLO, and remains a powerful player in Middle East politics.[21]

Hamas had its beginnings in 1967 as a wing of the Muslim Brotherhood. In 1978, the same organization was registered with Israeli authorities as a nonprofit, religious organization under the name, 'al Mujama,' under the leadership of Sheikh Ahmad Yassin, who was also head of the Muslim Brotherhood in Gaza. At first, the new organization spent most of its time promoting Islamic views and winning support for the Islamic movement in Palestinian institutions, universities and mosques. Hamas, as it is currently organized, was founded in December 1987 just when the intifada (uprising) in the occupied territories was starting.[22]

Meyrav Wurmser the director of the Center for Middle East Studies at the Hudson Institute in Washington, D.C. has shown how the relationship between Hamas and Iran has evolved over time. He notes how initially the ties between Iran and Hamas were marginal but began to grow stronger after Iraq's defeat in Gulf War I. Iran's ties to Hamas grew stronger after October 1992, when a Hamas delegation led by Dr. Musa Abu Marzook visited Tehran for meetings with key Iranian figures, including the Islamic Republic's supreme leader, Ayatollah Ali Khameinei. According to some reports, "Iran pledged an annual $30 million subsidy to Hamas, in addition to a promise of weapons and advanced military training at revolutionary guard facilities in Iran, Lebanon, and Sudan."[23]

In November 2006, Hamas had announced that the Iranian government had given Hamas over $120 million[24] with Iran pledging more financial and political support in the future.[25] "The alliance with Hamas is a key part of Iran's larger Levant strategy whereby it acquires powerful regional clients to sow the seeds of the Islamic revolution. This strategy is intended to bring Iran one step closer to establishing a caliphate that would spearhead a pan-Islamic jihad against the West, most notably the United States and Israel."[26]

It's 1938 All Over Again

Ever since the Islamic revolution in 1979, Iran and Israel have been bitter enemies and relations between Iran and Israel have been filled with tension and discord. The tension between the two nations was ratcheted up several notches with the election of President Mahmoud Ahmadinejad in the summer of 2005. Since his election in 2005, Mahmoud Ahmadinejad has been a vocal and outspoken critic of Israel and he has often called for the tiny nation's destruction.

In October of 2005, speaking to an audience of about 4,000 students at a program called "The World Without Zionism," President Ahmadinejad stated that Israel would be "wiped off the map" and that attacks by Palestinians would destroy it.[27] In April 2006, he lashed out at the Jewish state by declaring it "a rotten, dried tree" that could be knocked over by "a single storm." He continued his tirade by saying, "The existence of the Zionist regime is tantamount to an imposition of an unending and unrestrained threat so that none of the nations and Islamic countries of the region and beyond can feel secure from its threat."[28] In June of 2007, Ahmadinejad stated that, "With God's help, the count-down button for the destruction of the Zionist regime has been pushed by the hands of the children of Lebanon and

Palestine...By God's will, we will witness the destruction of this regime in the near future."[29]

Beside his virulent anti-Semitism, Mahmoud Ahmadinejad has also been an ardent denier of the Holocaust that saw six million Jews slaughtered by the Nazis during World War II. He has called the Holocaust "a myth," and a "legend" that was "fabricated . . . under the name 'Massacre of the Jews'", and has requested that the Jews living in Israel be "extirpated from the Middle East map and moved to some German or Austrian province."[30]What is most disconcerting about Mahmoud Ahmadinejad is not his anti-Semitism, but rather his apocalypticism that is leading him and Iran towards the development of nuclear weapons that he could in turn launch against Israel.

The Apocalyptic President

Mahmoud Ahmadinejad, the fourth child out of seven children, was born Mahmoud Saborjhian in the town of Aradan, about 80 miles southeast of Tehran to a blacksmith father and finally moving to Tehran when he was a year old. His strong religious beliefs surfaced at an early age in large part due to his very religious mother. She dresses in an all-embracing black chador and insists on the rigid separation of the sexes never sitting next to a man that was not a close relative.[31]

In 1976, he took Iran's nationwide university entrance exams and entered Iran University of Science and Technology (IUST) as an undergraduate student of civil engineering. Ahmadinejad continued his studies in the same university, entering the Master of Science program for civil engineering in 1984, the year he joined the Islamic Revolutionary Guards Corps, and in 1987 received his Ph.D. in traffic and transportation engineering and planning.[32]

Following the 1979 Islamic revolution, he became a member of the ultra-conservative faction of the Office for Strengthening Unity (OSU), tasked with achieving that goal between Universities and Theological Seminaries. The OSU was established by Ayatollah Mohammad Beheshti, one of Khomeini's key collaborators, to organise Islamist students against the rapidly growing Mojahedin-e Khalq (MeK).[33]

President Ahmadinejad is a devout Shia Muslim from the Jamkaran region that lies just south of Tehran the capitol city of Iran. It is from this region in Iran where many Shia Muslims believe that the 12th Imam, Abul-Qassem Mohammed, will return from his "occultation" to lead Islam in triumph over its enemies. "Veneration of the 12th Imam is common among Iran's 68m population, whose religious practices mix piety, respect for learned clerics and age-old mysticism."[34] He "has not only reached out to millions of pious Iranians through venerating the 12th Imam, but has engaged with deeply conservative religious groups that shunned politics for much of the 26 years of the Islamic Republic."[35]

Ahmadinejad's presidency has been one that has been very apocalyptic and he has placed a special emphasis on the 12th Imam. "One of the first acts of Mr. Ahmadinejad's government was to donate [$20 million] to the Jamkaran mosque, a popular pilgrimage site where the pious come to drop messages to the Hidden Imam into a holy well."[36] It was also rumored that he had plans to link Jamkaran with Tehran, nearly 100 miles away, with a high-speed rail link enabling the politicians to get to the mosque in double-quick time.[37]

As a devout Shia Muslim, Mahoud Ahmadinejad believes in the soon return of the 12th Imam, also known as the Mahdi, which he believes is his divine mission to bring to fruition. In his first speech before the UN in September 2005, he concluded his speech by calling on God to hasten the return of the Imam: "O mighty Lord, I pray to you to hasten the emergence of your last repository, the promised one, that

23

perfect human being, the one that will fill this world with justice and peace."[38] "In a widely circulated video, which has been depicted as an example of Ahmadinejad's excessive religious devotion, he is heard telling a leading ayatollah of having felt "a light" - coming from the imam – while giving his fiery speech September 2005 regarding Iran's nuclear program at the United Nations."[39] At a theology conference later that year, Ahmadinejad declared, "The most important task of our revolution is to prepare the way for the return of the Twelfth Imam."[40]

Ahmadinejad is not shy about discussing or sharing his beliefs on the 12th Imam: "His name is known and he will emerge and establish justice in the world," Mr. Ahmadinejad told a recent press conference. I'm proud of this belief. It's not just a religious belief, it's very progressive. A belief in the 12th imam is a belief in the world of tomorrow."[41] His beliefs in the 12th Imam are so strong that, Mahmoud Ahmadinejad "has put the hidden imam's long-awaited return at the heart of his political philosophy in a manner not exhibited by his predecessors."[42]

The return of the Imam Mahdi is the most significant event in the future for the Shiite faithful and has thunderous eschatological consequences. This return will occur shortly before the Final Judgment and the end of history. Imam Mahdi will return at the head of the forces of righteousness and do battle with the forces of evil in one, final, apocalyptic battle. When evil has been defeated once and for all, the Imam Mahdi will rule the world for several years under a perfect government and bring about a perfect spirituality among the peoples of the world.[43] Twelver Shiism is, then, a deeply eschatological religion. Important to understanding Shia religious belief is the understanding that the end of time will be preceded by an era of perfect justice and spirituality. The world, for the Shiite, is a deeply immoral, degenerate, and corrupt place; these are the necessary preludes to the appearance of Imam Mahdi.[44] This is vitally important in understanding Shia culture and political theory. Most of Iranian history can only be understood in relationship to the Doctrine of Return and the prophecies associated with it.[45] Mr. Ahmadinejad is close to the messianic Hojjatieh Society, which is governed by the conviction that the 12th Imam's return will be hastened by "the creation of chaos on Earth." He has fired Iran's most experienced diplomats and scores of other officials, presumably those who don't share his belief in the apocalyptic conflagration."[46]

In early 2006, the London Telegraph reported that unnamed Western officials suspect the Iranian president of instigating a clash with the West in the hope of rekindling the spirit of Islamic revolution and speed up the arrival of the Hidden Imam. Some pundits suspect that the Iranian president is purposely trying to nudge the Hidden Imam out of his hidey-hole — to "influence the divine timetable," as the Telegraph put it — thus his maniacal need for enriched uranium, in order to "destroy the world to make it right."[47]

Adding to the apocalypse-now interpretation, German political scientist Matthias Kuntzel in a recent New Republic article points to Ahmadinejad's glorification of martyrdom: "Is there an art that is more beautiful, more divine, more eternal than the art of the martyr's death?" the president asked in an early post-election interview. Princeton historian and Middle East specialist Bernard Lewis makes it clear where the president's religiously inspired end-times thinking might lead: "Ahmadinejad and his circle are in an apocalyptic mood," Lewis says. "The use of a nuclear weapon wouldn't bother them in the least."[48]

Iran's March Toward Nuclear Armament

In November 2004, the CIA submitted and released its yearly 721 report to Congress in accordance with the Intelligence Authorization Act passed in 1997. This report detailed Iran's pursuit toward nuclear weapons: [49]

"The United States remains convinced that Tehran has been pursuing a clandestine nuclear weapons program, in contradiction to its obligations as a party to the Nuclear Non-proliferation Treaty (NPT). During 2003, Iran continued to pursue an indigenous nuclear fuel cycle ostensibly for civilian purposes but with clear weapons potential. International scrutiny and International Atomic Energy Agency (IAEA) inspections and safeguards will most likely prevent Tehran from using facilities declared to the IAEA directly for its weapons program as long as Tehran remains a party to the NPT. However, Iran could use the same technology at other, covert locations for military applications.

Iran continues to use its civilian nuclear energy program to justify its efforts to establish domestically or otherwise acquire the entire nuclear fuel cycle. Iran claims that this fuel cycle would be used to produce fuel for nuclear power reactors, such as the 1,000-megawatt light-water reactor that Russia is continuing to build at the southern port city of Bushehr. However, Iran does not need to produce its own fuel for this reactor because Russia has pledged to provide the fuel throughout the operating lifetime of the reactor and is negotiating with Iran to take back the irradiated spent fuel."[50]

The report goes on to state how Iran was receiving assistance in its nuclear ambitions from the father of Pakistan's atomic bomb A.Q. Khan. From the available record, Khan sold nuclear technology, including weapons blueprints and uranium enrichment equipment, to a rogue's gallery of target states—North Korea, Syria, Iraq, Libya—if the country had the multimillions required. Khan visited each country to make available his extensive expertise of trafficking in the world's underground nuclear smuggling network. Instead of being turned over to an international tribunal for justice, Khan was permitted to retire into semiprivate life in Pakistan, evidently secure with the hundreds of millions he had been paid for his services since around 1990.[51]

According to the NCRI (National Council of Resistance of Iran), as far back as sometime between 1994 and 1996, Khan provided Iranian nuclear scientists with the blueprints of a Chinese-designed warhead. Moreover, the NCRI claimed that in 2001 Khan provided the Iranians with a quantity of highly enriched uranium, perhaps not enough to make a bomb, but still a sizable quantity. What Khan's confession and the subsequent revelations made clear was that the Iranians had access through Khan to key design information and weapons-grade uranium, breakthrough elements Iran would need if it were to build a bomb.[52]

The Evidence Against Iran

In spite of Iran's claims that their nuclear program is for peaceful purposes, there is plenty of evidence to suggest that a more sinister plan is intended. In September of 2004, Iran began converting 37 tons of uranium yellowcake into uranium hexafluoride gas. Though Iran called the yellowcake a test amount, experts said the 40 short tons could produce enough fissile material for several weapons. Iran argued that its uranium-enrichment program was intended to produce low-enriched uranium for use the nation's 1,000-megawatt nuclear power plant that it began constructing in the 1970's.[53]

The United States, however, has countered Iran's claims of peaceful purposes for its nuclear program. The United States has argued that Iran is "sitting on top of perhaps one quarter of the world's known oil reserves, with sufficient natural gas and oil to provide electric power for more than four generations of Iranians. Iran's estimated 26.6 trillion-cubic-meter natural gas reserve is the second largest in the world. By comparison to oil and gas, nuclear power is expensive."[54] The United States sees Iran's arguments as being deceptive and a way of concealing their true intentions for obtaining nuclear technology with the sole purpose being to transfer that technology for weapons purposes.

Iran's Nuclear Facilities Exposed

In a mid-August 2002 press conference held in Washington D.C., the National Council of Resistance of Iran (NCRI) exposed Iran's clandestine nuclear activities. During this press conference, the NCRI revealed the secret Natanz uranium enrichment facility. According to the NCRI, as of August 2002, the project had cost 95 billion toumans ($9.6 million). Funding had been provided by the Supreme National Security Council and was outside of the supervisory purview of the Budget and Planning Organization. The Natanz facility is reportedly located 100 miles north of Esfahan, which not so coincidentally, is where Iran's largest nuclear research center, The Nuclear Technology/Research Center, is located. On December 12, 2002 the Institute for Science and International Security (ISIS), having acquired satellite imagery of the Natanz site, released an issue brief stating its concern "the capability to make separated plutonium and highly enriched uranium, the two main nuclear explosive materials" in spite of Iran's strong objections that the Natanz facility was intended to generate electricity.

During the press conference, the NCRI also revealed the existence of the Arak facility. It was revealed that the Arak facility that was being built appeared to be designed to produce heavy water, which is needed to moderate the chain reaction for plutonium enrichment and not uranium enrichment like the facility at Bushehr. According to information provided by the Iranian authorities, after the revelation of the Arak facility, the Iranian heavy water reactor program consisted of two different facilities: the heavy water production plant at Arak and the 40 MW(th) IR-40, construction of which was planned to start at Arak in 2004. The revelation of the Arak facility cast serious doubt about Iran's claims that its nuclear ambitions were for peaceful purposes but rather nuclear armaments.[55]

Iran Admits The Obvious

In *Jerusalem Countdown* Hagee states, "Iran has been engaged in a pattern of clandestine activity that has concealed weapons work from International Inspectors. Technology and scientist from Russia, China, North Korea, and Pakistan have propelled Iran's nuclear program much closer to producing a bomb than Iraq ever was."[56] He was breathlessly telling his readers that his sources were informing him that Iran could have a bomb by April 2006.

> "My sources in Israel support this information. As I was preparing the first release of this book, they told me (April 2005) that Iran was in stage 5 and can have a bomb ready in twelve to eighteen months. That would make Iran's nuclear weapons ready by April 2006 unless international diplomacy prevails."[57]

In April 2006, Ahmadinejad announced boldly to the world that Iran had "joined the club of nuclear countries" by successfully enriching uranium for the first time. Ahmadinejad announced it at a nationally televised ceremony that was clearly aimed at drumming up support for the nuclear program. He addressed an audience that included top military commanders and clerics in an ornate hall in one of Iran's holiest cities, Mashhad. Before he spoke, screens on the stage showed footage of nuclear facilities and scientists at work. "At this historic moment, with the blessings of God Almighty and the efforts made by our scientists, I declare here that the laboratory-scale nuclear fuel cycle has been completed and young scientists produced enriched uranium needed to the degree for nuclear power plants Sunday," Ahmadinejad said. "I formally declare that Iran has joined the club of nuclear countries," he said. The crowd broke into cheers of "Allahu akbar" or "God is great" As part of the ceremony, costumed dancers performed on the stage, holding aloft vials of raw uranium and also chanting "Allahu akbar."[58]

He has also struck a very defiant tone regarding Iran's nuclear program vowing that Iran will not stop its nuclear work. For countries wanting Iran to halt its nuclear work, he said, "Our answer to those who are angry about Iran obtaining the full nuclear cycle is one phrase, we say: "Be angry and die of this anger."[59] In a live televised speech in the holy city of Mashhad, Ahmadinejad reiterated his defiant tone:

"Iran is a nuclear country and if you continue your mischief, Iran will tomorrow conquer higher summits ... It will punch you (the West) in the mouth ... The Iranian nation will go on its way with power and will not stop until it conquers all the summits of honor... If you think you can make the Iranian nation refrain from its resolute will through sanctions and heavy economic pressures, you are wrong."[60]

His defiance has even led him to call for the destruction and annihilation of the West. "Our objective is to annihilate all corrupt powers that dominate our planet today...Our enemies do not fear the technological, economical and industrial aspects of our nuclear program but tremble at the thought of the Islamic republic sitting as equals with them at the same table." Ahmadinejad also said that the West should repent, "otherwise Iranians will hoist their flag on the roof of their buildings."[61]

Iran's Foreign Minister Manouchehr Mottaki has echoed Ahmadinejad's defiant tone regarding Iran's enrichment activities. In an address at Iran's University of Science and

Technology he stated, "Tehran will not halt its uranium enrichment activities" adding that the policies being pursued by the United States and the United Nations sanctions "is doomed to fail."[62]

In spite of new U.N. sanctions calling, for "mandatory travel bans" "asset freezes for specific Iranian officials"[63] that also "bans trade with Iran in goods which have both civilian and military uses"[64] President Ahmadinejad remains undaunted in his long-term goal of Iran reaching the full nuclear cycle.

On December 17, 2007, Iran received its first shipment of nuclear fuel needed to power the Bushehr plant. On January 28, 2008 Irina Yesipova, a spokeswoman for Russia's state Atomstroiexport company in charge of building Iran's nuclear plant, said the eighth and final shipment of 9.5 tons of uranium fuel had been delivered to Iran.[65] With this last shipment of nuclear fuel, "Russia has delivered more than 132 tons of uranium fuel to Iran since Dec. 17."[66] Iran has said Bushehr, the country's first nuclear reactor, will begin operating in the summer of 2008, producing half its 1,000-megawatt capacity of electricity.[67]

In addition, in December 2007, Iran indicated that it was building a second nuclear power plant. The revelation came in comments by Iran's Atomic Organization, Gholamreza Aghazadeh: "We are building a 360-megawatt indigenous power plant in Darkhovein," he said, referring to a southern city north of Bushehr. Aghazadeh stated that Iran needed to increase the centrifuges at the Natanz enrichment plant from 3,000 to 50,000, saying that with the current 3,000, it could only produce fuel for a 100-megawatt plant.[68]

Israeli Defense Minister Ehud Barak has stated that Israel suspects Iran is quite advanced in its nuclear work and has started work on fashioning a nuclear warhead. "We suspect they are probably already working on warheads for ground-to-ground missiles... Our interpretation is that clearly the Iranians are aiming at nuclear capability," he said. "It's probably true that ... they may have slowed down the weapons group in 2003, because it was the height of American militarism...[but] are quite advanced, much beyond the level of the Manhattan Project."[69]

Unidentified diplomats reported in April 2008 that Iran had assembled more than 300 advanced centrifuges, the sophisticated IR-2, in its underground enrichment plant at Natanz. One of the unidentified diplomats confirmed that Iran had started linking up advanced centrifuges in a configuration used for enrichment. Iranian officials confirmed that they had started using the IR-2 centrifuge that can churn out enriched uranium at more than double the rate. Their reports underlined Iran's determination to push ahead with its enrichment program despite U.N. Security Council sanctions.[70]

Not long after this report was announced, Iran upped the ante by announcing that it had begun to install thousands of new centrifuges for uranium enrichment. Ahmadinejand announced that Iran was installing 6,000 new centrifuges at its Natanz underground enrichment facility.[71]

On the day of the Annapolis conference in December 2007, Iran tested a newly developed ballistic missile with a range of 2,000 kilometers (1243 mi), which is capable of reaching Israel, US Army bases in the Middle East and eastern European cities, including Moscow.[72] Iran has also taken receipt of the North Korean BM-25 surface-to-surface missile that were purchased as part of a comprehensive deal with North Korea. The BM-25 is based on outdated technology of the Russian SSm6, a missile launched from submarines and has a range of 1,550mi, and are capable of carrying nuclear warheads.[73]

Israel is also concerned that Teheran is developing a cruise missile that can evade interception by the Arrow, the IDF's anti-ballistic missile defense system. Iran is suspected of having smuggled Ukrainian X-55 cruise missiles and using them as models for an independent, domestic project. A cruise missile, which flies at low altitudes to dodge radar detection and interception, could be used to carry a nuclear warhead.[74]

According to an intelligence report, Iran plans to arm its Shahab-3 missiles with nuclear warheads. The report said it was code-named Project 111 and that the "aim is arming Shahab-3 missiles with nuclear warheads."[75] Just recently, Iran announced that it was able to launch a rocket into space that it had built in just nine months[76] and had intentions to launch more rockets into space in the future.[77] These revelations by Iran only heighten the concerns of Western nations that Iran is fast tracking towards nuclear armament.

The U.S. in February 2008 "shared sensitive information with the International Atomic Energy Agency on key aspects of Iran's nuclear program that Washington says shows Tehran was directly engaged in trying to make an atomic weapon. The decision by the U.S. administration to declassify its intelligence and indirectly share it with Iran through the IAEA was a clear reflection of Washington's drive to pressure Iran into admitting that it had focused part of its nuclear efforts toward developing a weapons program."[78] China followed suit and provided the U.N with intelligence on Iran's nuclear ambitions. The information that was turned over to the U.N.'s nuclear watchdog, the International Atomic Energy Agency (IAEA) centered on information Iran had obtained from China on blueprints for shaping uranium metal into warheads, on how to manufacture nuclear-armed weapons, explosives used to detonate radioactive material, and the procurement of dual-use technology.[79]

Iran's nuclear threat has so worried Israel that the Israeli Air Force (IAF) "has been conducting an increasing number of training missions outside of Israel, over the Mediterranean, in the United States, Canada, Italy and other countries."[80]

The Unstoppable Force vs. The Immoveable Object

In 1981, the tiny nation of Israel perfectly executed an audacious attack against Iraq's Osirak nuclear reactor destroying it. Many military analysts credit this attack for the overwhelming success that the coalition forces enjoyed in securing Kuwait's freedom from Iraqi occupation during Operation Desert Storm in 1991-1992. If Israel had not acted when it did, many feel that coalition forces would have been staring down the barrel of a nuclear-armed Iraq making the invasion a near if not an outright impossibility. Iran took special note of this and did not repeat Iraq's mistake. Their multiple nuclear facilities are spread out throughout the country and have been built underground to ensure that any attack against them would be difficult to destroy.

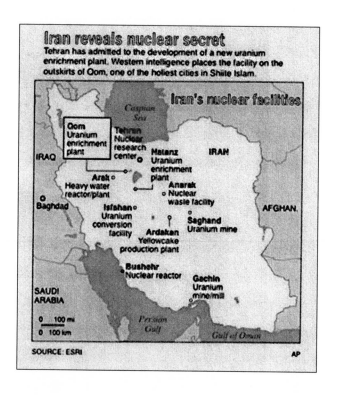

"Most analysts agree that Iran has diversified its nuclear technology infrastructure over an estimated three hundred sites, possibly many more. One strategy at play here may be defense oriented: a large number of sites geographically distributed are more difficult to attack."[81]

Because Iran's nuclear sites are spread throughout the country and buried deep underground, making it extremely difficult to attack and thus degrade in a conventional attack, the Bush administration in 2006 was said to be making plans to destroy Iran's nuclear sites using low yield nuclear bombs. The plans, presented to the White House by the Pentagon entailed the use of B-2A Stealth bombers armed with the nuclear bunker busting B61-11earth penetrating warheads.[82] These bombs have the ability to penetrate 20 feet into dry earth and can produce a shock wave sufficient to crush a bunker buried beneath 100 meters of layered rock.[83]

Now reports have surfaced that Iran may be trying to modernize certain parts if its military force in the anticipation of an Israeli or American preemptive strike on its nuclear facilities. Iran has turned to none other than Russia and China in order to modernize an air force that is woefully outdated. The Russian Kommersant Daily reported that an Iranian aviation company agent had confirmed that China would export to Iran 24 J-10A fighters between 2008 and 2010 at a price of $1 billion.[84] In a report that appeared in the Navy Times, Iran was in negotiations with Russia to buy 250 state-of-the-art fighter jets. The report went on to state how "top Israeli defense officials were investigating the potential Iran-Russia deal, in which Iran would pay $1 billion for about a dozen squadrons' worth of Sukhoi Su-30 "Flanker" fighter-bombers. As a part of the deal, Iran would also buy aerial tanker planes that could extend the fighters' range."[85]

If it acquired the Flankers, Iran would enjoy a quantum leap forward in its air power capability. Iran has invested much of its resources in surface-to-air missile defenses, but its fighter fleet currently consists of decades-old American exported F-14 Tomcats and F-4 Phantoms to go along with a hodgepodge of 1970s-era Russian fighters, including Su-25 "Frogfoots," and newer models, including the MiG-27 "Flogger."[86]

Iran's air force is not the only aspect of its military apparatus that it is trying to upgrade. In December 2008, there were media reports that Russia had begun supplying Iran's military with the S-300 surface to air missile batteries. "Israel and the United States fear that, were Iran to possess S-300 missiles, it would use them to protect its first nuclear power plant now under construction at Bushehr by Russian contractors. That would make any potential military strike on the plant much more difficult."[87]

Notes

[1] Andrew Higgins, "A Texas Preacher Leads Campaign To Let Israel Fight," *Wall Street Journal* (July 27, 2006), p.A1

[2] This information was accessed from the John Hagee Ministries website on 6/30/06 and at the time of this writing could not be verified from the sources provided. However, in a July 27 2006 Wall Street Journal article by Andrew Higgins titled *A Texas Preacher Leads Campaign To Let Israel Fight* states that the book had sold over 700,000 copies.

[3] Dave Eberhart, "Pastor John Hagee's D.C. Meeting Worries Jews," *NewsMax* (May 17, 2007): http://archive.newsmax. com/archives/articles/2007/5/16/211015.shtml

[4] John Hagee, "Back Cover", *Jerusalem Countdown: A Warning to the World* (Lake Mary, FL: Frontline, 2006)

[5] John Hagee, "Back Cover", *Jerusalem Countdown: A Prelude to War* (Lake Mary, FL: Frontline [2006], 2007)

[6] John Hagee, "Introduction", *Jerusalem Countdown: A Warning to the World* (Lake Mary, FL: Frontline, 2006)

[7] Steve Holland, "McCain rejects pastor's backing after Hitler remark," *Reuters* (May 22, 2008): http://www.reuters. com/article/Print?articleId+USN2252526620080522

[8] Helen Gray, "Armageddon: Soon?," *The Kansas City Star* (September 23, 2006), p.E16

[9] Dave Eberhart, "Pastor John Hagee's D.C. Meeting Worries Jews"

[10] Alexandra Alter, "For some evangelicals, Mideast war stirs hope," *Miami Herald* (August 08, 2006), p.A1

[11] Joyce Ibrahim, "Iran and Terrorism," *Woodrow Wilson International Center for Scholars* (September 14, 2006): http://eisenhowerseries.com/pdfs/terrorism_ob/final/final_2006_09-14.pdf

[12] Mortimer B. Zuckerman, "Moscow's Mad Gamble," *U.S. News & World Report Vol. 140, No. 4* (January 30, 2006/ February 6, 2006), p. 76

[13] Jerome R. Corsi, Atomic Iran: How the Terrorist Regime Bought the Bomb and American Politicians (Nashville, TN: WND Books, 2005), p.130

[14] Daniel L. Byman, "Proxy Power: Understanding Iran's Use of Terrorism," *Brookings Institute* (July 26, 2006): http://wwww.brookings.edu/opinions/2006/026iran_byman. aspx?p=1

[15] Dr. Daniel Byman, "Iran, Terrorism, and Weapons of Mass Destruction," *Brookings Institute: Studies in Conflict & Terrorism* 31 (March 2008), p.171-172 http://tinyurl. com/yerfuvc

[16] Haynes, "Hezbollah is making trouble in Iraq, says US," *The Times* (July 3, 2007), p.30

[17] ibid, p.30

[18] Michael R. Gordon, "Hezbollah Trains Iraqis in Iran, Officials Say," *New York Times* (May 5, 2008): http://tinyurl. com/44kzdl

[19] ibid

[20] Jerome R. Corsi, *Atomic Iran*, p.136

[21] http://www.globalsecurity.org/military/world/para/hamas. htm

²² http://www.globalsecurity.org/intell/library/reports/crs/ 931014-hamas.htm

²³ Meyrav Wurmser, "The Iran-Hamas Alliance, http://tinyurl. com/ydgttoz

²⁴ http://www.iranpressnews.com/english/source/017682.html

²⁵ http://english.aljazeera.net/news/middleeast/2007/03/200 8525122240439340.html

²⁶ Meyrav Wurmser, "The Iran-Hamas Alliance",

²⁷ Nazila Fathi, "Wipe Israel 'off the map' Iranian says," *International Herald Tribune* (October 25, 2005): http:// www.iht.com/articles/2005/10/26/news/iran.php

²⁸ Angus McDowall, "Ahmadinejad speech inflames tension," *The Independent UK* (April 15, 2006), p.30

²⁹ "Iran president sees "countdown" to Israel's end", *Reuters* (June 3, 2007): http://www.reuters.com/article/worldNews/ idUSBLA32653020070603?feedType=RSS&rpc=22

³⁰ Charles Krauthammer, "In Iran, Arming for Armageddon," *Washington Post* (December 16, 2005), p.A35

³¹ Robert Tait, "A humble beginning helped to form Iran's new hard man," *The Guardian UK* (July 2, 2005):http:// www.guardian.co.uk/world/2005/jul/02/iran.roberttait

³² http://tinyurl.com/yaqj334

³³ http://www.globalsecurity.org/military/world/iran/ahma-dinejad-bio.htm

³⁴ Najmeh Bozorgmehr and Gareth Smyth, "Second coming for imam is first concern for Iranian president: The religious

beliefs driving Mahmoud Ahmadi-Nejad have alarmed many clerics", *Financial Times*, (November 9, 2005), p.9

[35] ibid, p.9

[36] Anton La Guardia, "Divine Mission' driving Iran's new leader," *Telegraph UK* (January 15, 2006), p.10

[37] Adrian Levy and Cathy Scott-Clark, "War Games," *The Guardian UK* (December 8, 2007) http://www.guardian.co.uk/world/2007/dec/08/iran.cathyscottclark

[38] Masood Farivar, "Armageddon and the Mahdi: How Ahmadinejad is giving Shiite Islam a scary name", *The Wall Street Journal Online* (March 16, 2007): http://opinionjournal.com/taste/?id=110009796

[39] Robert Tait, "Iran: President leads the faithful awaiting return of 12th imam," *The Guardian UK* (February 21, 2006), p.23

[40] "Shias await the return of the Twelfth Imam," *The Irish Times* (August 4, 2006), p.12

[41] Robert Tait, "Iran: President leads the faithful awaiting return of 12th imam,"

[42] ibid

[43] http://www.wsu.edu:8080/~dee/SHIA/HIDDEN.HTM

[44] ibid

[45] ibid

[46] Arnaud de Borchgrave, "The Apocalyptic Vision of Iranian President Ahmadinejad," *NewsMax* (Feb. 9, 2006): http://archive.newsmax.com/archives/articles/2006/2/8/154740.shtml

[47] Christopher Orlet, "Apocalyptic Ahmadinejad," *The American Spectator* (October 6, 2006), n.p.

[48] Jay Tolson, "Aiming for Apocalypse", *U.S. News & World Report Vol. 140, No. 19* (May 22, 2006), p.34-35

[49] Jerome R. Corsi, *Atomic Iran*, p.25

[50] Unclassified Report to Congress on the Acquisition of Technology Relating to Weapons of Mass Destruction and Advanced Conventional Munitions, 1 July Through 31 December 2003; https://www.cia.gov/library/reports/archived-reports-1/july_dec2003.htm#iran

[51] Jerome R. Corsi,, *Atomic Iran*, p.40

[52] ibid, p.41

[53] Craig Smith, "Iran Moves Toward Enriching Uranium," *New York Times* (September 22, 2004): http://www.nytimes.com/2004/09/22/international/middleeast/22iran.html

[54] Jerome R. Corsi,, *Atomic Iran*, p.35

[55] http://www.globalsecurity.org/wmd/world/iran/natanz.htm

[56] John Hagee, Jerusalem Countdown, p.5

[57] ibid, p.8

[58] "Iran Claims to Have Successfully Enriched Uranium," *Fox News* (April 12, 2006) http://www.foxnews.com/story/0,2933,191334,00.html

[59] "Iran defiant over nuclear plans," *BBC* (April 13, 2006): http://news.bbc.co.uk/2/hi/middle_east/4905918.stm

[60] "Iran to defy West on nuclear: Ahmadinejad", *Agence France Presse*, (April 9, 2008): http://www.breitbart.com/article.php?id=080409190818.1goyp76k&show_article=1

[61] "Iran: President wants to 'annihilate corrupt powers,'" http://www.adnkronos.com/AKI/English/Security/id=1.0.2058939507

[62] "Mottaki: Iran will not halt uranium enrichment," http://www.iranfocus.com/modules/news/article.php?storyid=14325

[63] Patrick Worsnip and Louis Charbonneau, "Iran to face more travel bans, asset freezes: draft," *Reuters* (January 25, 2007): http://news.yahoo.com/s/nm/20080125/ts_nm/iran_sanctions_un_dc

[64] "New Iran sanctions target some civilian goods," *Associated Press* (March 3, 2008): http://www.cnn.com/2008/WORLD/asiapcf/03/03/iran.un.ap/index.html

[65] Report: Russia Completes Shipment of Uranium to Iran," *Fox News* (January 28, 2008): http://www.foxnews.com/story/0,2933,325906,00.html

[66] Jerome R. Corsi, "Nuke agency says Iran continuing weapons work," *WorldNetDaily* (February 26, 2008): http://www.worldnetdaily.com/index.php?pageId=57452

[67] "Iran gets 5th shipment of nuclear fuel," (January 22, 2008): http://tinyurl.com/yzns4ow

[68] Nazila Fathi, "Iran indicates it is building another nuclear plant," *International Herald Tribune* (December 17, 2007): http://www.iht.com/articles/2007/12/17/africa/17iran.5.php#end_main

[69] "Israel suspects Iranians already working on nuclear warhead," *Agence France Press* (January 26, 2008): http://afp.

google.com/article/ALeqM5hRl1Dbc3m8le0IY4P01L1_
KE5T8g

[70] George Jahn, "Diplomats: Iran Assembling Centrifuges," *Associated Press* (April 3, 2008): http://abcnews.go.com/International/wireStory?id=4583894

[71] "Iran starts installing new nuclear centrifuges," *Agence France Presse* (April 8, 2008): http://www.breitbart.com/article.php?id=080408124437.k89rrp7e&show_article=1

[72] "Iran tested new missile during summit," *Jerusalem Post* (December 12, 2007): http://tinyurl.com/2ruu3h

[73] Benny Avni, "New Iran Missiles Can Hit Europe," *New York Sun* (April 28, 2006), p.1

[74] Yaakov Katz and Herb Keinon, "Israel: Iran could have nukes by '09," *Jerusalem Post* (May. 6, 2008): http://tinyurl.com/ylsbbqw

[75] "Iran said to step up plans for Shahab missiles," http://www.iranian.ws/cgi-bin/iran_news/exec/view.cgi/7/13850

[76] Nasser Karimi, "Iran Built Space Rocket in Just Months," *Associated Press* (February 26, 2008): http://www.breitbart.com/article.php?id=D8V29LOO0&show_article=1

[77] "Iran plans to launch two more rockets into space", *Agence France Presse* (February 11, 2008):http://www.breitbart.com/article.php?id=080211114616.z25xjjg2&show_article=1

[78] George Jahn, "US Intel Links Iran With Nuke Bomb Bid," *Associated Press* (February 14, 2008): http://www.breitbart.com/article.php?id=D8UQ49R00&show_article=1

[79] Damien McElory, "China reveals Iran's Nuclear secrets to UNA," *The Telegraph UK* (April 4, 2008), p.19

[80] Hana Levi Julian "IAF: Training Abroad for the 'Real Thing,'" *Israel National News*

(December 17, 2007): http://www.israelnationalnews.com/News/News.aspx/124600

[81] Jerome R. Corsi, *Atomic Iran*, p.33

[82] http://www.globalsecurity.org/org/news/2006/060409-nuclear-strikes-iran.htm

[83] http://www.globalsecurity.org/wmd/systems/b61-11.htm

[84] Andrei Chang, "Analysis: China eyes J-10A sale to Iran," *United Press International* (December 14, 2007): http://www.upi.com/International_Security/Industry/Analysis/2007/12/14/analysis_china_eyes_j-10a_sale_to_iran/9163/

[85] Philip Ewing, "Reports: Iran may buy 250 jets from Russia," *Navy Times* (August 7, 2007): http://www.navytimes.com/news/2007/07/navy_iran_fighters_070730w/

[86] ibid

[87] http://www.foxnews.com/story/0,2933,470886,00.html

CHAPTER TWO

Russia:
A Superpower Rises Again

—ɯ—

Russia is back on the international stage. After a decade of eroding political and economic power, the domestic economy flourishes and, as state budget revenues grow, so do egos in the Kremlin and Russia's global aspirations. The Russian resurrection is mainly attributed to high oil prices, which have enabled the country to overcome the 1998 meltdown, to maintain an average rate of economic growth of 6.7 percent for the past decade, and to build a $1 trillion economy, the basis of its new strength.[1] Between 2002 and 2003 Russia's "GDP grew 7.3%, up from 4.3% in 2002, and inflation was 12%, down from 15.1% in 2002.

Other indicators also look good: the external debt to GDP ratio has fallen to 30% from 100% shortly after the August 1998 crash. Real incomes are rising even faster than GDP, growing by 9.8% year on year (August 2003 figures), and estimates of those living below the poverty threshold have fallen from 30% to 25% since 2000."[2]

As of 2006 Russia's "GDP has almost trebled, from $345bn in 2002 to $984bn in 2006, in dollar terms (partly due to economic growth, but also because the value of the ruble has soared). The economy is now growing at almost 7% per year - up from less than 5% four years ago. Inflation, meanwhile, has slipped from almost 16% in 2002 to single-digit figures. Exports have trebled - largely thanks to metals, oil and gas - to about $300bn, by far outpacing import growth. This has enabled Russia to pump up its foreign cash reserves. In 2002, the reserves stood at $44bn. By 2006, they had ballooned to more than $295bn."[3] This economic boom has lead to a dramatic increase "of so-called "high net worth individuals" - people whose spending power exceeds $1M - in Russia rose 15.5% - compared with an 8% swelling in their number globally, according to the Merrill Lynch and CapGemini World Wealth Report."[4]

Another benefit of record high oil prices is that it has allowed Russia to pay off the debt of the former Soviet Union. The Soviet Union left a huge debt after its collapse. Russia became the only country to inherit not only the foreign property of the former Soviet Union, but all of its foreign debts as well. It was extremely hard for Russia to serve the debt because the economy was declining steadily in the beginning of the 1990s. The Soviet debt had been restructured four times before the default of 1998. By 1999, Russia managed to either write off or delay the payments to private creditors (the London Club, for instance). However, such a compromise proved to be impossible with the Paris Club of Creditors. World prices on oil literally saved Russia from another financial catastrophe. Oil prices have been rising very fast since the beginning of the new century, which gave Russia an opportunity to complete major payments ($17 billion) to the Paris Club in 2003. As a result, Russia has become one of the most solvent countries of the world.[5]

Russia's Return To Authoritarianism

President Putin has been sending very strong signals that he intends to reassert Russia's influence in international affairs, including the Middle East, to a level it has not enjoyed since the downfall of the Soviet Union. By all appearances coming from Russia, it seemed that former President Vladimir Putin intentions was to move Russia further and further away from the democratic reforms, instituted by his predecessor Boris Yeltsin. Putin seemed to be moving to a more authoritarian style of government that was somewhat reminiscent of the former Soviet Union. As president, Putin's first move was to target the Russian oligarchs and their massive wealth and influence.

After the fall of the Soviet Union in 1991, Russia began to reform its economy that had been left a train wreck by the communist Soviet government. Under Boris Yeltsin, Russia began to move away from the command economy during the communist period and to a more capitalist free market economy. It allowed well-connected businessmen to purchase privatized state assets at extremely cheap prices thus becoming oligarchs.

Putin's first target was Mikhail Khodorkovsky, the former head of the Yukos oil company. Before his arrest in October 2003 on tax evasion charges, Khodorkovsky was considered to be Russia's richest man and one of Russia's leading oligarchs. According to Forbes magazine, Mikhail

Khodorkovsky's estimated wealth was close to $15 billion. Like many of the other Russian oligarchs, Khodorkovsky had amassed his fortune through the privatization of post-Soviet state assets. His arrest came hot on the heels of his activities in the political arena, including the acquisition of the rights to publish the prestigious Moskovskiye Novosti newspaper, and his hiring of a leading investigative journalist highly critical of Putin. It seems his political activism attracted the Kremlin's ire, with Mr. Putin apparently feeling threatened. Or at least that is what Mr. Khodorkovsky's supporters claim. They insist his arrest is the Kremlin's way of punishing Mr. Khodorkovsky for his political activities and for his failure to toe the Kremlin line - a claim Mr. Putin has angrily rejected.[6]

Another Russian oligarch that became the target of Putin's wrath was Mikhail S. Gutseriev, the former owner of one of Russia's largest private oil companies Russneft. Mr. Gutseriev stated that he was selling Russneft "to an investor loyal to the Kremlin", accusing "the government of President Vladimir V. Putin of forcing him out of the company using trumped-up tax claims." Mr. Gutseriev maintained that the government was using regulatory pressure on both foreign and domestic producers as a pretext to expropriate oil and natural gas property privatized in the 1990s, as part of an effort to effectively nationalize the energy industry.[7]

Another Russian oligarch, Leonid Rozhetskin, may have suffered the same fate that befell Mikhail Khodorkovsky and Mikhail Gutseriev. According to Joseph Farah's G2 Bulletin, "Britain's intelligence services – MI5 and MI6 – are spearheading the manhunt for a Russian-born media magnate who was an outspoken critic of the murder of Alexander Litvinenko, the former KGB spy poisoned by polonium."[8] It seems that he was kidnapped from his Latvian mansion home in Riga by "a specialist Russian hit team, made up of former KGB assassins, that has been mobilized to deal with Putin's opponents."[9]

Other than Yukos, the state's most significant plans for taking control of private property center on Gazprom, one of the country's largest companies and steward of the world's largest natural gas reserves. After selling off shares over the years, the state holds 37 percent of the company. The Russian government also planned to buy back just over 13 percent, worth about $5.3 billion, to retake a majority share. Some analysts at the time said Putin's Kremlin is planning to make Gazprom the nation's dominant energy company, akin to state-owned oil firms in the Middle East.[10]

Aside from the Yukos case, the government has suspended plans to privatize parts of Unified Energy Systems, the state-owned electricity monopoly; repeatedly put off auctioning a controlling stake in Svyazinvest, a major state-owned telecommunications firm; and failed to follow through on promises to lift foreign ownership restrictions on Gazprom, the state-controlled natural gas monopoly.[11] Putin appeared to be creating a hybrid between the command economy of the communist period and the free-market economy ushered in by his predecessor, Boris Yeltsin, according to analysts.

Rather than further liberalizing the market, Putin moved to impose his own rules and collect a greater share of industry's profits through taxation.[12]

After the Beslan school massacre in September 2004, that saw over 300 people killed, including 186 children, Putin started to implement measures that would begin to centralize the Russian government's authority. Under his plan, Putin would appoint all governors to create a "single chain of command" and allow Russians to vote only for political parties rather than specific candidates in parliamentary elections. Putin characterized the changes as enhancing national cohesion in the face of a terrorist threat, while critics called them another step toward restoring the tyranny of the state 13 years after the fall of the Soviet Union.[13]

The plan was the latest move in a five-year campaign by Putin to consolidate power and neutralize potential opposition in the new Russia. Since coming into office at the end of 1999, Putin's government had taken over or closed all independent national television channels, established unrivaled dominance of both houses of parliament, reasserted control over the country's huge energy industry and jailed or driven into exile business tycoons who defied him.[14] These moves by Putin were hailed by his political opponents as "the beginning of a constitutional coup d'état" and a "step toward dictatorship."[15]

In parliamentary elections that were held in December 2007, Putin's United Russia party took 70 percent of the seats in the new legislature ensuring he remained Russia's de facto leader even after he leaves.[16] His successor Dmitry Medvedev, was handpicked by Putin and is seen by many as a Putin protégé who will continue Putin's policies.[17] During the Russian presidential election Medvedev said, "I think that it will be a direct continuation of that path which is being carried out by President Putin."[18] He is expected to rule in concert with his mentor, an arrangement that could see Putin calling the shots despite his constitutionally subordinate position as Russia's prime minister.[19]

Even though the "new" Russia does not resemble the old Soviet Russia, many feel that "a new autocracy now governs Russia. Behind a facade of democracy lies a centralized authority that has deployed a nationwide cadre of loyalists that is not reluctant to swat down those who challenge the ruling party.[20] Given Putin's moves to centralize the authority of the Russian government and calling "the collapse of the Soviet Union as "the greatest geopolitical catastrophe" of the 20th century,"[21] it has lent credence to the feelings that Russia is returning to its Soviet past. As billionaire Boris Berezovsky, now living in political exile, stated, "It's definitely [gone] way back to the Soviet Union. Not in the sense of ideology, but in the sense of the organization of power."[22]

A Return To The Cold War

After coming to power, Putin embarked on a mission to restore the Russian military's prowess and prestige. He not only increased Russia's military spending budget, which has nearly quadrupled since he became president, but under his presidency, Russia has returned to its military tactics of the Cold War.

When Putin became president, he inherited a military with low morale along with dilapidated and aging equipment. He embarked on a spending spree in a bid to return Russia's military back to respectability. In 2005, Russia's defense spending increased by 22%, in 2006 it increased by 27%, and in 2007 it was estimated to increase by as much as 30%. According to Jane's Sentinel Country Risk Assessments, the Russian shopping list includes two new submarine-launched nuclear ballistic missiles, the Bulava and the Sineva, both with a 5,000 mile range and capable of carrying 10 nuclear warheads, and a new anti-aircraft missile, the S-400, which the Russian ministry of defense claims is effective against incoming missiles. It also plans to spend heavily on the new TU-160 strategic bomber, which can launch cruise missiles, the SU-34 "Fullback" fighter-bomber capable of all-weather attacks on heavily defended targets and a new fifth-generation fighter, the Sukhoi T-50, which was expected to come into service in 2008 as Russia's main lightweight front-line fighter.[23]

In a move reminiscent of the Cold War, in the fall of 2008, Putin announced that Russia would have its long-range nuclear bombers resume sorties in international airspace. The U.S. Navy intercepted two Russian TU-95 Bears as they approached the USS Nimitz and the guided missile cruiser USS Princeton at an altitude of 2000 feet in the western Pacific.[24]

Since July 2007, there have been at least eight instances where Russian aircraft have been intercepted near U.S. airspace. U.S. aircraft deployed from Elmendorf Air Force Base off the coast of Alaska handled the eight documented interceptions; according to a U.S. official familiar with the situation.[25] These over flights have not been limited to the U.S. alone. Russian long-range bombers have also been intercepted as they were nearing British and Norwegian airspace.

Russia's navy has also returned to its Soviet roots by returning to Cold War navy patrols. For the first time since the fall of the Iron Curtain, Russia plans to re-operate the Tartus and Latakia ports in Syria as permanent bases for the Russian Navy in the Mediterranean basin, according to recent western media reports. Rumors on the growing Russian activity in the Mediterranean began spreading following a statement by Russian Navy commander, Admiral Vladimir Masorin, as he visited the Russian Navy base in the Sebastopol port in Ukraine. "Being present in the Mediterranean is very important for our Navy in the Black Sea," the admiral said.[26] Russia has long been talking about reviving a permanent naval base in the Mediterranean. During the Cold War, the Soviet navy had a permanent presence on the Mediterranean, using the Syrian port of Tartus as a supply point.[27] Just as recently as August 2009, the Pentagon detected two Russian-attack submarines patrolling several hundred miles off the East coast of the United States.[28]

In another example of Russia flexing its muscles militarily, Russia has been very active in showing off its nuclear capabilities. In the fall of 2007, the Russian navy test-fired a series of its new Bulava-M long- range nuclear missiles claiming further tests of the latest experimental series would take place by 2008.[29] This was followed by Russian bombers test-firing missiles in the Bay of Biscay off the French and Spanish Atlantic coasts.[30] The success of these tests has made an increasingly assertive Russia to threaten that it could use nuclear weapons in preventive strikes to protect itself and its allies.[31]

In a move that was eerily reminiscent of the Cold War era, Russia, in a Victory Day celebration in May 2008, put its military hardware on display in the Red Square for the first time since the demise of the Soviet Union. More than

100 combat vehicles, including intercontinental ballistic missile launchers, rolled across the cobblestone Red Square and strategic bombers and fighter jets roared overhead in the first such display in 18 years. Most of the combat vehicles shown in the Victory Day parade were slightly modernized versions of Soviet weapons designed in the 1980s.[32] The return of the Russian military back to apparent respectability has fostered an attitude of strength and boldness. "Russia is back, so beware of us," says Sergei Strokan, a journalist with Kommersant. "Don't touch us. We are strong enough."[33]

Back In The Arms Business

For decades, the Americans and the Soviets competed fiercely for global influence by supplying warplanes, missiles, and tanks to opposing sides in conflicts worldwide. But when the Soviet Union collapsed in 1991, Russia's weapons industry fell into disarray. Now, Russia is back in the arms business, with surging orders from countries across the globe. Reviving defense exports has been a good way to boost international respect for Russia. It is considered good business.

Russian arms sales have risen steadily since 2001, the year after Putin came to power, and was estimated to reach

$7.5 billion in 2007. Russia is now the world's No. 2 arms exporter, after the U.S., which sold some $21 billion in weapons in 2006. These exports deals included a $3 billion deal with "Venezuelan President Hugo Chavez who ordered 100,000 Kalashnikov rifles, 24 Sukhoi Su-30, and 53 military helicopters"[34] and a deal in February 2007 in which India inked an agreement with Russia to purchase 40 Sukhoi Su-30 fighter jets for $1.6 billion.[35] India, along with China, are Russia's biggest customers and between the two of them they "have accounted for 70% of Russia's arms-export revenues since 2001."[36]

Russia has also been busy arming Israel's archenemy to the north Syria. In 2005, Russia sold Syria its advanced anti-aircraft missiles the Igla SA-18.[37] Fast forward three years and Russia is at it again by allowing Syria to purchase "Russia's S-300 surface-to-air missile defense shield, which is similar to the U.S.-funded, Israeli engineered Arrow antimissile system currently deployed in Israel. The S-300 system is being run not by Syria but by Russian naval technicians who work from Syria's ports, security officials said."[38] However, Syria is not the only archenemy of Israel to benefit from Russia's arms business. So has Iran.

Since 1992, Russia has sold Iran hundreds of major weapons systems, including twenty T-72 tanks, ninety-four air-to-air missiles, and a handful of combat aircraft like the MiG-29. Moscow also plans to upgrade Tehran's Su-24, MiG-29 aircraft, and T-72 battle tanks.[39] Russia was scheduled to deliver in the fall of 2006 "29 Tor M1 radar-guided anti-aircraft missile launchers to Iran, in a deal valued at $700 million."[40] In late December 2007, it was reported that Russia was going to supply Iran with the S-300 surface-to-air missile defense shield. This new anti-aircraft system, designed by Russia in the 1970's is supposed to be capable of shooting down American or Israeli fighter jets in the event of any strike on Iran's nuclear facilities. With a range that is supposed to be superior to that of the U.S. Patriot system, the S-300 has the capability "of shooting down aircraft, cruise missiles and ballistic missile warheads at ranges of nearly 100 miles, and at altitudes of up to 90,000 feet" [41] significantly enhancing Iran's air defense ability.

Russia's Strategic Regional Partners

In Russia's continuing move towards reasserting itself on the world stage, Russia has been busy establishing alliances and partnerships with countries in its region. Three nations that seem to be getting extremely close to Russia are China, India, and Iran.

In 2005, China and Russia held joint military exercises as a demonstration of cooperation against the perceived U.S. hegemony in the region.[42] Two years later China and Russia held joint military exercises that were organized by the Shanghai Cooperation Organisation (SCO) that is seen by some as a rival to the North Atlantic Treaty Organization (NATO). The SCO was founded as a nonmilitary alliance in 2001 to combat drugs and weapons smuggling as well as terrorism and separatism in the region. It has since developed a role in regional trade and is increasingly regarded by Moscow and Beijing as a counterweight to US global influence. Russian officials have also proposed an alliance between the SCO and a body representing most of the former Soviet republics.[43]

China's neighbor to the south India has also benefited from a cozy and warm relationship with Russia. India-Russia relations have been traditionally based on a broad convergence of interests. Formal cooperation between India and Russia began in 1960, when the two countries agreed to a program of military-technical cooperation, which culminated in a formal alliance in 1971. Since the Treaty of Peace, Friendship and Cooperation of that year, Soviet power ensured substantial economic, political and military cover for India during the Cold War. India's military inventories are still composed largely of Russian-made weapon systems. Recent statistics indicate that India was the leading buyer of Russian made arms in 2005. At present, acquiring advanced foreign technologies and licensing the manufacture of military equipment are receiving priority in Indian military imports. Again, Russia is the leading partner of India in this sphere. A successful model of this type of collaboration is BrahMos Aerospace, a $300 million Indo-Russian joint venture to manufacture 1,000 supersonic cruise missiles over the next decade for domestic and export markets. As India's Defense Research and Development Organization looks to market several of its products internationally, military-technical cooperation with Russia's state-owned Rosoboronexport, which performs the international activity for the Russian defense industry, could greatly improve India's chances of making a dent in the highly competitive global arms bazaar.[44]

Out of all of the strategic partnerships that Russia has struck with the nations in its region the one that has been most alarming and disconcerting is its nuclear deal with Iran to build the Bushehr nuclear power plant and supply it with the nuclear fuel it needs in order to become operational.

The reactor units at Bushehr were initially built by a German company, Siemens, and were built to a plan closely resembling that of the Biblis A unit in Germany. The Bushehr I reactor was 85 percent complete and the Bushehr II reactor was partially complete prior to the 1979 Iranian Revolution, after which construction of both reactors halted. Ayatollah Khomeyni declared this project "anti-Islamic," and the government of Mehdi Bazargan soon abandoned it. In January 1995, Russia and Iran signed a contract under which Russia would provide one light water reactor at Bushehr that would be similar in configuration to a Russian plant at Balakovo, Saratov.[45] Russia sees the Bushehr reactor as a mammoth civilian venture, an estimated $800 million to $1 billion nuclear power project that adheres to international norms, brings home cash, and ensures close relations with the Islamic regime in Tehran.[46]

Therefore, should Israel decide to take preemptive action against Iran's nuclear facilities, like it did Iraq's Osirak in 1981, it could be more than plausible for Russia to lead a military coalition that would include Iran to come against

Israel in retaliation considering Russia's huge investment in Iran's nuclear facilities.

It seems that what John Hagee laid out in his book *Jerusalem Countdown* is unfolding right before our very eyes.

For the first time in history, some of the nations described in Ezekiel's prophecy are making front-page headline news.

The Gog/Magog war of Ezekiel 38 and 39 seems as if it is about to finally be fulfilled.

Or is it...

Notes

[1] Andreas Goldthau, "Resurgent Russia? Rethinking Energy Inc.," *Policy Review* No. 147 (February/March 2008), p.53

[2] http://www.propertyfrontiers.com/countries/russia/economy.html

[3] Jorn Madslien, "Russia's economic might: spooky or soothing?," *BBC*, (July 4, 2007): http://news.bbc.co.uk/go/pr/fr/-/2/hi/business/6265068.stm

[4] ibid

[5] "Russia pays off USSR's entire debt, sets to become crediting country," *Pravda* (August 22, 2006): http://english.pravda.ru/russia/economics/84038-paris-club-0

[6] "Profile: Mikhail Khodorkovsky," *BBC* (June 16, 2006): http://tinyurl.com/yj4uqe4

[7] Andrew E. Kramer, "Russian Oil Magnate Forced to Sell to Putin Loyalist, He Says," *New York Times* (July 31, 2007), p.C4

[8] http://www.worldnetdaily.com/index.php?pageId=59930

[9] ibid

[10] Peter Baker, "Putin's Kremlin Asserting More Control of Economy: Yukos Case Reflects Shift on Owning Assets, Notably in Energy," *Washington Post* (July 9, 2004) p.A14

[11] ibid

[12] ibid

[13] Peter Baker, "Putin Moves to Centralize Authority," *Washington Post* (September 14, 2004) p.A01

[14] ibid

[15] ibid

[16] Vladimir Isachenkov, "Putin's Party Wins Russian Election," *Associated Press* (December 3, 2007): http://apnews.myway.com/article/20071203/D8T9VK2O0.html

[17] "Russians look for continuity in Putin ally Medvedv," *Associated Press* (March 2, 2008): http://www.usatoday.com/news/world/2008-03-02-russia-election_N.htm

[18] Christian Lowe, "Russia's Medvedev vows to pursue Putin policies," *Reuters* (March 2, 2008): http://www.reuters.com/articlePrint?articleId=USL2883523820080302

[19] Vladimir Isachenkov, "Putin, Medvedev Pledge Unified Path: Putin, Medvedev Say Apparent Win for Kremlin's Candidate Means Continuity in Russia," *Associated Press* (March 2, 2008): http://abcnews.go.com/print?id=4372855

[20] Clifford Levy, "Putin's Iron Grip on Russia Suffocates Opponents," *New York Times* (February 24, 2008), p.A1

[21] "Putin deplores collapse of USSR", *BBC* (April 25, 2005): http://news.bbc.co.uk/go/pr/fr/-/2/hi/europe/4480745.stm

[22] Jim Maceda, "Putin's 'sovereign democracy' looks familiar. Putin's near-autocratic power resembles the old Soviet Union to opponents," *NBC News* (March 30, 2007), http://www.msnbc.msn.com/id/17876775/

[23] Gethin Chamberlain, Tim Shipman and Nick Holdsworth, "Vladimir Putin rearms his Cold War military" *Telegraph UK* (August 20, 2007), p.29

[24] "U.S. Navy Intercepts Russian Bombers Flying Near Ships," http://www.foxnews.com/story/0,2933,330362,00.html

[25] Sara A. Carter, "U.S. assessing Russian flyovers," *The Washington Times* (February 13, 2008), p.A09

[26] Aryeh Egozi, Alex Fishman, "Russian Navy to operate from Syria," (August 6, 2007): http://www.ynetnews.com/articles/0,7340,L-3434145,00.html

[27] Guy Faulconbridge, "Russian navy to start sorties in Mediterranean," *Reuters* (December 6, 2007): http://tinyurl.com/ygsum4t

[28] Luis Martinez, "Why Are Russian Subs Patrolling Off East Coast of U.S.?" (August 5, 2009): http://abcnews.go.com/News/story?id=8257819&page=1

[29] "Russian Navy announces plans to test-fire nuclear missiles," http://www.earthtimes.org/articles/show/90417.html

[30] "Russian bombers to test-fire missiles in Bay of Biscay," *TimesOnline* (January 22, 2008): http://www.timesonline.co.uk/tol/news/world/europe/article3230615.ece

[31] Steve Gutterman, "Russia: Could Use Nuclear Weapons", *Associated Press* (January 19, 2008): http://ap.google.com/article/ALeqM5i1fg9K4w_OQvYX65kemvhiOOJTZAD8U92Q881

[32] Vladimir Isachenkov, "Russia puts tanks and missiles back in Red Square parade," *Associated Press* (May 9, 2008): http://news.yahoo.com/s/ap/20080509/ap_on_re_eu/russia_victory_day

[33] Jim Maceda, "Putin's 'sovereign democracy' looks familiar. Putin's near-autocratic power resembles the old Soviet Union to opponents."

[34] Jason Bush, "Russia's Back in the Arms Game," *Business Week*, (April 10, 2007): http://www.businessweek.com/globalbiz/content/apr2007/gb20070409_470397.htm

[35] http://www.indianaviationnews.net/airshow

[36] ibid

[37] Inigo Gilmore, "Israel acts to halt Russian missile deal with Syria," *Telegraph UK* (January 13, 2005), p.12

[38] Aaron Klein, "Syria in 'furious' frenzy to get Russian missiles," *WorldNetDaily* (February 06, 2008):http://www.worldnetdaily.com/index.php?pageId=55612

[39] http://www.cfr.org/publication/11869/#2

[40] Jason Bush, "Russia's Back in the Arms Game"

[41] Luke Harding, "Russia will supply new anti-aircraft missiles for Iran," *The Guardian UK* (December 27, 2007), p. 26

[42] Peter Finn, "Chinese, Russian Militaries to Hold First Joint Drills," *Washington Post* (August 15, 2005), p.A10

[43] Tony Halpin, "'Rival to Nato' begins first military exercise," *TimesOnline* (August 6, 2007), p.32

[44] Zorawar Daulet Singh, "Reviving the India-Russia partnership," *Asia Times Online*, (November 14, 2006) http://www.atimes.com/atimes/South_Asia/HK14Df01.html

[45] http://www.globalsecurity.org/wmd/world/iran/bushehr-reactor.htm

[46] Scott Peterson, "Russian nuclear know-how pours into Iran," *The Christian Science Monitor* (June 21, 2002): http://www.csmonitor.com/2002/0621/p01s03-woeu.html

CHAPTER THREE

A 'Who's Who List' of Gog and His Confederates

—ɯ—

"Few if any prophecy scholars question that the potential fulfillment of this text comes in the end times and that Russia and her allies will go down to the little nation of Israel "to take a spoil" (Ezekiel 38:13, KJV)."[1]

Tim LaHaye and Jerry B. Jenkins *Are We Living in the End Time*

In December 2006, an end-times related article was circulating through the Internet creating a small buzz especially in discussion boards that are dedicated to biblical prophecy. The reason why it was creating a buzz was because it was written by Ines Ehrlich who is the editor of *Ynetnews.com* the online version of one of Israel's leading daily's the *Yediot Aharonot*. The article was titled "Modern day Gog/Magog: Similarities between Ezekiel's prophecies, today's Mideast reality uncanny" and it echoed the same prophetic claims that Christian prophecy teachers have stated will happen:

> "Current world events are beginning to increasingly resemble the 2,500 year old bible prophecy made by Ezekiel in chapters 38-39. Ezekiel foresaw the rise of Russia (or Turkey, depending on the interpretation) in a coalition with Iran and other Middle Eastern countries (Sudan, Ethiopia and Libya)."[2]

What made this so interesting is that a familiar and often taught end-times paradigm was now being reported in Jewish news sources. Another Gog/Magog article that was published in Israel National News followed this article. The article, written by Ezra HaLevi, had a map showing the familiar alignment of nations that are to come against Israel during the Gog/Magog invasion. It seems as if the Jews have finally understood what Ezekiel was prophesying all those many millennia ago.

Then again, one could argue that it really was not much of a surprise that it would create such a stir. This interpretative version of Ezekiel 38 and 39 has become so accepted that no one questions it. This is the contention of Timothy J. Dailey. In his book *The Gathering Storm* he wrote that the Russian led invasion of Israel is "so commonly held as to be almost taken for granted...So ingrained is this theory that books on biblical prophecy have assumed routinely over the years that it was beyond doubt. Without discussing the evidence, for example, John Walvoord simply concluded that the description in Ezekiel 38 and 39 "could only refer to what we know today as Russia." What is the evidence for this commonly held belief? In truth, the Russian invasion theory rests upon scanty foundations indeed."[3] "Because so many people believe that dispensationalism is basically true, they believe that competing systems must stay within the general parameters of dispensationalism to be considered orthodox"[4]

You see, prophecy teachers such as John Hagee would have us believe that all Bible scholars and expositors either took or take the position that Russia is the Gog of Ezekiel 38 and 39.[5] The notion that there is a consensus amongst Bible scholars and expositors that agrees with the view that Russia will fulfill her end-times role, as Gog in Ezekiel 38 and 39 is debatable. History has borne out that there have been many nominees for Gog throughout the centuries. It reads almost like a 'Who's Who List.'

Historical Interpretations of Ezekiel 38 & 39

Throughout the centuries, Bible scholars and expositors have interpreted Ezekiel 38 and 39 based on the geopolitical events of their day. Every time the geopolitical landscape changed, so did the identity of the end-time player of Ezekiel 38 and 39. Francis Gumerlock in his book *The Day and the Hour: Christianity's Perennial Fascination with Predicting the End of the World* has done a great job chronicling the history of Christianity's failed attempts at predicting the future century after century. He has also chronicled the various Gog/Magog candidates down through the halls of time.

In the fourth and fifth centuries, it was the Goths and the Moors.[6] In the sixth and seventh centuries, the Goths and the Moors were replaced by the Huns and the Avars.[7] In the eighth century, the Huns were replaced by the Islamic

Empire.[8] In the tenth century, the Hungarians replaced the Islamic empire[9] and in the eleventh century, the Hungarians were replaced by the Avars who were also identified by Theodore of Syncellus in the seventh century as being the end-time Gog and Magog.[10] In the fourteenth century, it was the Tartars (Mongols) and the persecutors of the Lollards.[11] The sixteenth century saw multiple nominees. They were the Saracens, the Turks, the Mohammedans and the Papacy.[12]

This was the view that was supported by such biblical luminaries as Martin Luther and Thomas Newton. Martin Luther "saw in the Turks the fulfilment of the prophecy of Ezekiel and the Revelation of St. John about Gog and Magog, and therewith a judgment of God for the punishment of corrupt Christendom."[13] Luther "identified the papacy as the antichrist and the Turk as the very devil incarnate."[14] For Martin Luther the world was coming to an end, Christ's return was imminent, and he saw the Turks and the papacy supporting "each other against Christ and his kingdom."[15]

Thomas Newton like Luther before him saw the Turks (Ottoman Empire) as fulfilling the events of Ezekiel 38 and 39. Thomas Newton in his book *Dissertation on the Prophecies Which Have Remarkably been Fulfilled at This*

Time Are Fulfilling in the World commenting on Gog/Magog wrote the following:

"In Ezekiel there is a famous prophecy concerning 'Gog and Magog,' and this prophecy alludes to that in many particulars. Both that of Ezekiel and this of St. John remain yet to be fulfilled; and therefore we cannot be absolutely certain that they may not both relate to the same event, but it appears more probable that they relate to different events. The one is expected to take effect before, but the other will not take effect till after the millennium. 'Gog and Magog' in Ezekiel are said expressly, xxxviii. 6, 15. xxxix. 2. to come from ' the north quarters' and' the north parts,' but in St. John they come from' the four quarters or corners of the earth.' 'Gog and Magog' in Ezekiel bend their forces against the Jews resettled in their own land, but in St. John they march up against 'the saints' and church of God in general. 'Gog and Magog' in Ezekiel are with very good reason supposed to be the Turks, but the Turks are the authors of 'the second woe, and the second woe,' xi. 14. 'is past before the third woe, and the third woe,' long precedes the time here treated of. Ezekiel's prophecy apparently coincides with the latter part of the eleventh chapter of Daniel, and presignifies the destruction of the Othman empire, which includes Gomer and many European, as well as Ethiopia, Libya, and other nations."[16]

In the seventeenth century, the Pope Spain and the Native Americans became the nominees that replaced the Saracens, Turks, and Mohammedans.[17]

In the early nineteenth century, a new candidate had been identified to fulfill the events of Ezekiel 38 and 39. That person was Napoleon Bonaparte. An early nineteenth century English periodical called *The Gentleman's Magazine* in its October 16, 1816 edition identified Napoleon Bonaparte as Gog who was leading the forces of France (Magog) against Russia which dwelled in the "the Land of unwalled villages."[18]

Here is how the author justifies this interpretation:

"Now several circumstances in the account of this expedition agree so particularly with what Ezekiel prophesied two thousand five hundred years ago, of certain enemies of the church of God under the name of "Gog of the Land of Magog" and which prophecy the Apostle St. John shews in the Book of Revelation not to have come to pass in his time, but to be still future...Gog, in this prophecy, is represented as a "chief

Prince of Meshech and Tubal," who are mentioned, in the book of Genesis, as two sons of Japhet, by whose posterity Europe was peopled. The great agent then in these troubles must be expected to be a European Power, and one of the principal of them, "a Chief Prince." And this description accords with France, which has long been one of the most powerful of them, and a general Disturber of the world.

That Russia is the other Country intended in this Prophecy, there seems no room to doubt, since no other Country answers so well to the account here given of it. It is called the Land of unwalled Villages...Now no country appears to have so few great Towns in it as Russia; and that it abounds in Villages must be inferred from two accounts which I have met with respecting it."[19]

"In the view of the author, Russia is the Christian good guy and France the antichristian bad guy! France was considered to be an enemy of the church after its many antichristian policies and actions during its revolutionary years. Napoleon did nothing to change these opinions. Russia was considered to be nominally Christian. The war between the two nations was in the news, and like today, the headlines were driving the interpretation of the Bible. And, of course, Russia is "north" of France."[20]

Toward the end of the nineteenth century, a new candidate would emerge after Napoleon's defeat and it would turn out to be a bear of a nominee.

The View of the Classics

The great and classic Bible expositors like Matthew Henry and Adam Clarke did not agree with John Cumming and his view on Russia being the end-times bad guy of Ezekiel 38 and 39. Matthew Henry in his commentary on Ezekiel believed that the events in Ezekiel 38 and 39 were fulfilled in the Maccabean War against Antiochus Epiphanes IV. He states, "This chapter, and that which follows it, are concerning Gog and Magog, a powerful enemy to the people of Israel, that should mount an offensive against them, but their army should be routed and their scheme defended; and this prophecy, it is most probable, had its accomplishment after the return of the people of Israel in the struggles they had with the kings of Syria, especially Antiochus Epiphanes, or in some other way."[21]

Like Matthew Henry, Bible commentator Adam Clarke sees the fulfillment of Ezekiel 38 and 39 in the Maccabean War against Antiochus Epiphanes as well. Consider the following comments by Clarke on verses in Ezekiel 38 and 39:

"This is allowed to be the most difficult prophecy in the Old Testament. It is difficult to us, because we know not the *king* nor *people* intended by it: but I am satisfied they were well known by these names in the time that the prophet wrote.

I have already remarked in the *introduction* Ezekiel 1:1 to this book that there are but *two* opinions on this subject that appear to be at all probable: 1. That which makes GOG *Cambyses*, king of *Persia*; and, 2. That which makes him ANTIOCHUS EPIPHANES, king of *Syria*. And between these *two* (for one or other is supposed to be the person intended) men are much divided...I shall at present examine the text by this latter opinion."[22]

Biblical commentators Jamieson, Fausset, and Brown took a view that was wholly different from that of Matthew Henry and Adam Clarke. They saw the events of Ezekiel 38 and 39 as a prophetic parable using real world events to describe the final battle between God and Antichrist. In writing the commentary on this section of Ezekiel, A.R. Fausset argues for a non-literal approach when interpreting Ezekiel 38 and 39 listing several reasons for this approach:

> "The objections to a *literal* interpretation of the prophecy are—(1) The ideal nature of the name Gog, which is the root of Magog, the only kindred name found in Scripture or history. (2) The nations congregated are selected from places most distant from Israel, and from one another, and therefore most unlikely to act in concert (Persians and Libyans, &c.). (3) The whole spoil of Israel could not have given a handful to a tithe of their number, or maintained the myriads of invaders a single day (Eze 38:12, 13). (4) The wood of their invaders' weapons was to serve for fuel to Israel for seven years! And *all* Israel were to take seven months in burying the dead! Supposing a million of Israelites to bury each two corpses a day, the aggregate buried in the hundred eighty working days of the seven months would be three hundred sixty millions of corpses! Then the pestilential vapors from such masses of victims before they were all buried! What Israelite could live in such an atmosphere? (5) The scene of the Lord's controversy here is different from that in Isa 34:6,

Edom, which creates a discrepancy. (But probably a different judgment is alluded to). (6) The gross carnality of the representation of God's dealings with His adversaries is inconsistent with Messianic times. It therefore requires a non-literal interpretation. The prophetical delineations of the divine principles of government are thrown into the familiar forms of Old Testament relations. The final triumph of Messiah's truth over the most distant and barbarous nations is represented as a literal conflict on a gigantic scale, Israel being the battlefield, ending in the complete triumph of Israel's anointed King, the Saviour of the world."[23]

Renowned 18th century Bible commentator and celebrated exegete Augustin Calmet, like the classical Bible commentators that came after him, viewed the events in Ezekiel 38 and 39 as being fulfilled in the past. Calmet, a Benedictine Monk, wrote several works on the Bible that was commended by both Catholics and Protestants during his time. He published a twenty-three volume work called *Commentary on the Bible* (1706-1716) and a seventeen volume work titled *Universal History* (1735). His *Historical and Critical Dictionary of the Bible* (4 vols. 1722-28) – the first work of its kind was translated into English, German, and other languages has passed through many editions.[24] Calmet believed that events of Ezekiel 38 and 39 refers to the time of the Persian king Cambyses the son of Cyrus the Great who succeeded him to the Persian throne in 530 B.C.[25]

Other Gog/Magog Nominee's

The editors of the *Encyclopaedia Biblica* list Mithridates VI of Pontus as fulfilling the role of Gog in Ezekiel 38. Mithridates VI was an easy and obvious choice. According to the editor's, Mithridates, whose rule extended over the area that was prophesied to be involved in the Ezekiel 38 and 39 assault against Israel, had conscripts in his military forces from Persia, Put, and Cush, and could muster these forces from his stationed region in the far north.

"Mithridates alone could rightly be entitled 'prince of Meshech and Tubal,' his seat of power being where the Moschi and the Tibarenes lived, and his sway extending over the territory once associated with those names. None could more aptly be considered as the coming Gog than the proud conqueror of Scythia who reigned over all the coast-lands of the Black Sea and brought from the farthest [north] his armies. No other ruler of these realms had with him Paras, Cush, and Put, Gomer, Togarmah, and the extreme [north] than Mithridates, whose general Pelopidas could justly boast of the Persian auxiliaries, Egyptian ships, Cappadocian troops, Armenian contingents, and Scythian, Sarmatian, Bastarnian, and Thracian hordes that swelled the king's forces...But in an age of eschatological hopes, the confidence could not fail that, should he invade the 'navel of the earth' where quiet prosperity had been restored, and prove indeed to be the predicted Gog, he would there met with a miserable end."[26]

Other likely Gog/Magog nominees have included Gyges king of Lydia and his descendants, the Babylonians, an Assyrian prince named Gagi, the Parthians and the Scythian invaders.[27]In spite of the assertions by modern day prophecy writers that "almost all expositors" agree with the Russian interpretive view of Ezekiel 38 and 39, as you can surely see, the Gog/Magog candidates have been quite varied.

View of the 20th century and Beyond

In the nineteenth century a new end-times bad guy would emerge that would take the place of the previously mentioned names and become entrenched in that position for the next one hundred plus years. The view that Russia was going to lead an end-time coalition against the restored nation of Israel in fulfillment of Ezekiel 38 and 39 was codified by C.I. Scofield in his reference Bible *The Scofield Reference Bible*,[28] popularized by Hal Lindsey and his book *The Late Great Planet Earth*,[29] and finally went mainstream with the release of the *Left Behind* series by Tim LaHaye and Jerry Jenkins. This view has been further solidified in the psyche of prophetic thought with the publication of such works as the aforementioned *Jerusalem Countdown: A Warning to the World*,[30] Joel Rosenberg's book *Epicenter: Why The Current Rumblings In The Middle East Will Change Your Future*,[31] and Mark Hitchcock's books *The Coming Islamic Invasion of* Israel[32] and *Iran: The Coming Crisis*.[33]

Although this view was very popular in the twentieth century (and now twenty-first century), its roots can in part be traced back to the the nineteenth century. For example, John Cumming a preacher and author of several prophecy related works during that time period, wrote about Russia's role as Gog in apparent fulfillment of Ezekiel 38 and 39. In his work *The End: The Proximate Signs Of The Close Of This Dispensation*, Cumming establishes who he believes will fulfill Ezekiel's foe from the north. In Lecture 7 of *The End* titled "The Russian Northern Confederacy" Cummings wrote:

> "Russia will burst forth, overcome all resistance, march to Palestine; and, there unsuccessful in achieving the evil thing it had set its heart upon, it will learn that God will avenge his own by the most terrific judgments, which are described in the next chapter as being poured out upon that guilty and ambitious confederacy."[34]

For Cumming there was no doubt in his mind that these northern peoples were indeed the Russians. For him it was "beyond all dispute" going so far as to assert, "commentators have no doubt and no difficulty about that."[35]

Russia became an easy target for prophecy watchers to fulfill the leading role as protagonist in fulfillment of Ezekiel 38 and 39. With the Bolshevik revolution in 1917, Russia became an atheistic and communist country that ultimately became a nation that was driven toward world domination and it is a nation that is "far north" of Israel.

Following the prophetic scenario of his predecessor's, Hal Lindsey laid out his prophetic scenario in his 1970's bestseller *The Late Great Planet Earth*. In his book Hal Lindsey stated, "Shortly after the restoration of the Jews in the land of Israel, an incredible enemy will arise to its "uttermost north." This enemy will be composed of one great nation, which will gather around it a number of allies. It is this "Northern Confederacy" that is destined to plunge the world into its final great war, which Christ will return to end."[36] This "Northern Confederacy" according to Lindsey was "Russia (USSR), Iran (Persia), Ethiopia or Cush (Black African Nations), Libya or Put (Arabic African Nations), Gomer and its horde (Iron Curtain Countries-Poland, East Germany, and Czechoslovakia), and Togarmah and all its horde (Southern Russia and the Cossacks)."[37]

Lindsey changed his prophetic scenario from his original outline in *The Late Great Planet Earth* when he published another prophecy related book titled *The 1980's: Countdown to Armageddon*. In *Countdown to Armageddon* Lindsey wrote, "In *The Late Great Planet Earth* I predicted that the Soviets would begin their Middle East campaign with a sweep through the Persian Gulf area into Iran. The recent Russian invasion of Afghanistan was a first step in that direction."[38] Lindsey went on to write that the Russian invasion of Afghanistan in 1979 "telegraphed the Soviet intention to take over the entire Middle East...This area has now fit precisely into the pattern predicted for it. All that remains is for the Russians to make their predicted move."[39] Lindsey continued: "Before Russia attacks Israel, however, it will first invade Iran, or Persia, as it is called in Ezekiel chapter 38, verse five. When we apply this prophecy to modern times, it becomes obvious that the Soviets will use their recent conquest of Afghanistan as a springboard to overthrow Iran and gain control of the Persian Gulf area."[40] Lindsey said nothing of this sort. In fact, in *The Late Great Planet Earth* he predicted that Russia and Iran would be allies:

"In order to mount a large-scale invasion predicted by Ezekiel, Russia would need Iran as an ally. It would be much more difficult to move a large land army across the Caucasus Mountains that border Turkey, than the Elburz Mountains that border Iran. Iran's general terrain is also much easier to cross than Turkey's"[41]

In *Planet Earth–2000A.D.*, released in 1994, Lindsey again changes his prophetic outline when he wrote, "The collapse of the Soviet state was absolutely necessary to the fulfillment of biblical prophecy."[42] In this book, you can also begin to witness a change in Lindsey's thinking on Russia's role in the fulfilling of this prophecy. He reverts somewhat to the earlier premise of *The Late Great Planet Earth* of a Russian/ Arab alliance that is to invade Israel except this time there is a new twist. Instead of Russia leading the invasion, it is a Muslim Confederation with Iran leading the group along with a reluctant Russia:

"In Ezekiel 38, the Bible describes the way Russia fulfills that role. Russia seems to be led into this conflagration **almost against her will**. I believe it will be the strong Islamic influence on Moscow that places those "hooks into the jaws" of Magog. What the Bible is talking about here is an alliance of Arab, African, and Islamic nations with the republic of Russia. Today Russia is being linked more and more closely to this emerging new Islamic world order than ever before. Iran, the leader of this Muslim confederation, is looking forward to the time when the Islamic world can draw Russia into an alliance against Israel."[43] (emphasis added)

Needless to say time, has not been kind to either Mr. Lindsey or the prophecy writers that preceded him. The predictions that they have laid down in their books have been proven to be less than accurate. In the years since the publication of books touting the Russia as Gog theory, "The Soviet Union no longer exists in its communist form; a rag-tag group of Afghan fighters beat the Russians in a miscalculated war; the once feared Russian army is only a shadow of its former self; Islamic terrorists shot Russian school children as they attempted to escape their captors; and the United States is playing a large role in rooting out Islamic terrorist groups."[44]

The Iron Curtain and communism were torn down with the collapse of the Berlin Wall in 1989. By 1991, the Soviet Union, the leader of the Gog/Magog invasion according to Lindsey, ceased to exist and the countries and satellite nations that once made up the Soviet Empire broke away and sought democratic reforms and eventually joined the European Union or have opened negotiations for entry into the European Union.

East and West Germany once separated by the Berlin Wall are now a unified Germany and has become a powerhouse in the European Union. The nations that once made up Czechoslovakia seceded from one another and Czechoslovakia, a shell of its former self, is now called the Czech Republic, and is a member of the European Union. Poland too has shed its communist past and in 2004 was one of ten nations that became a member of the ever-expanding European Union.[45] In December 2003, Libya announced that it was giving up on its weapons of mass destruction program and "agreed to disclose all its weapons of mass destruction and related programs and to open the North African country to international weapons inspectors to oversee their elimination."[46] Since this disclosure by the Libyan government, the U.S. began "restoring full diplomatic relations with Libya"[47] and began lifting "restrictions on air transport cooperation with Libya, including aircraft sales...and has established an embassy in Tripoli."[48]

In the spring of 2005, Russian President Vladimir Putin made the first visit ever by a Russian leader to the Jewish state due to the greatly improved Israeli-Russian relations over the past 15 years. While in Israel, he was to meet with then Prime Minister Ariel Sharon and other senior Israeli officials for talks on advancing Middle East peace talks.[49] While in Israel, President Putin made a visit to the Western Wall in the Old City. Of this visit by Putin Israeli then Vice

Premier Ehud Olmert said, "Considering the history of relations and the fact that there were times that we were on one side and Russia was entirely on the other side ... (the visit) indicates the significant change that took place between the two countries."[50]

Undaunted by these facts, books and articles that continue to promote a future invasion of Israel by Russia continue to be churned out at break neck speed. In a 2005 WorldNetDaily column, Hal Lindsey stated:

"Thousands of years ago, the prophet Ezekiel foretold the rise of a vast anti-Israeli alliance, spearheaded by Russia with Iran as its principle partner. Just in this generation, Iran has gone from being a pro-Western U.S. ally to one of America's most implacable enemies. Russia is currently Iran's principle protector and supplier of nuclear materials for what will most undoubtedly become part of Iran's nuclear arsenal.

The only alternative to a nuclear Iran would be an Israeli first strike against Iran's nuclear facilities. Ezekiel described exactly this situation more than 2,000 years ago, and now, for the first time in history, all the players are on the same stage at precisely the right moment in history for Ezekiel's vision to become reality."[51]

Now here we stand at the dawning of the twenty-first century and the prophetic landscape has once again changed and Islam (in the form of Iran) is now returning to again take the place that it once did in the eighth and sixteenth century as the prophesied end-time villain of Ezekiel 38 and 39. True to form, contemporary prophecy teachers are rewriting their prophetic outlines. In a February 2006 internet article on his old website titled Iran, Russia and Ezekiel, Lindsey writes that it is no longer Russia leading the Gog/ Magog battle but it is now Iran that is the leading protagonist invader of Israel. This article completes the change in Lindsey's view that began in 1994. The following is a quote from the article:

"The Hebrew prophet Ezekiel, writing from his vantage point in history, circa 537 BC, predicted that in the last days, there would be a great war involving not only Islam, but dragging an **unwilling** Moscow along for the ride, as if God had put 'hooks in its jaws', the prophet said. (emphasis added)

Leading the Islamic alliance, according to Ezekiel, is Persia, (modern Iran). Together with the Islamic nations of North Africa and the Mediterranean Middle East, Ezekiel says they will constitute an invasion force that will move against the nation of Israel."[52]

In the same article he further states, "In Ezekiel's day, there had been no nation called 'Israel' for almost two centuries and no sovereign nation called Israel would exist for another 2500 years. Today, in 2006, Israel exists, as Ezekiel predicted. Iran, [Persia] is Israel's sworn enemy, as Ezekiel predicted. The Islamic world is poised, waiting for an excuse to wipe Israel off the map, as Ahmadinejad is promising to do if Iran obtains nuclear weapons."[53]

Surely, you have noticed the obvious by now. Initially, it was Soviet Russia that was leading an alliance that was to invade Israel and now it is Iran, along with a reluctant Russia, that is leading an Islamic alliance against Israel over a *possible* Israeli pre-emptive strike against Iran's nuclear facilities. His view of Ezekiel 38 and 39 has changed over the last 30 plus years due to the changing nature of world events. As you can see, Hal Lindsey along with other prophecy prognosticators of the past have and are reading the events of Ezekiel 38 and 39 through the lens and backdrop of newspaper headlines.

Dr. Gary North in his publisher's preface to Dr. Dwight Wilson's updated version of his 1977 book *Armageddon Now! The Premillenarian Response to Russia and Israel Since 1917* [54]commented on how the failed communist coup of the Soviet Union on August 19 – 21, 1991 was the death knell (or at least it should have been) for not only this view but also for "popular dispensationalism" as he called it. "The failed *coup* placed a tombstone on top of a huge pile of utterly inaccurate prophecies made by the leaders of popular dispensationalism, a pile of errors that had been growing since 1917."[55] As he continued to note, "None of the pre-1989 books forecasted the fall of the Berlin Wall in 1989; none of the 1990 and 1991 books forecasted the failed Soviet *coup* of 1991. Were these two events relevant prophetically? If the answer is "yes," the paperback prophets should have foreseen both events. If the answer is "no," why were communism and Russia said for decades to be relevant prophetically? *These "experts" never foresee accurately; they merely revise retroactively.*"[56] Finally, he noted that with the collapse of the USSR dispensationalists would have to identify a new potential invader of the state of Israel or abandon dispenstionalism. Well instead of abandoning dispenstionalism, dispensationalists have done the very thing that Dr. North suggested they would do and they have nominated Iran as that potential invader.

But what happens if the United States or Israel acts preemptively against Iran and their nuclear facilities and military apparatus utterly destroying them all? Who will then take Iran's place? Will it be Syria? Syria may not be motivated given Israel's successful cross border bombing raid against its own secret nuclear facility.[57] Will it be Iraq? This too seems highly unlikely for the foreseeable future given that Iraq is a fledgling democracy that is continuing its democratic reforms to form the second stable democracy in the Middle East with Israel being the first. Could it be Turkey? This too seems highly unlikely given that Turkey is a NATO member and doing everything it can to draw closer to the European Union. However, given the latest round of prophecy books, it looks like they are quickly becoming the new nominee.

Only time will tell whom the next candidate to "fulfill" Ezekiel 38 and 39 will turn out to be. Whoever it turns out to be, they will become another nominee in a long list of 'Who's Who' Gog/Magog nominees.

Notes

[1] Tim LaHaye and Jerry B. Jenkins, *Are We Living in the End Times?: Current Events Foretold In Scripture...And What They Mean* (Carol Stream, IL: Tyndale House Publishing, 1999), p.85

[2] Ines Ehrlich, ""Modern day Gog and Magog: Similarities between Ezekiel's prophecies, today's Mideast reality uncanny", *ynetnews.com* (December 10, 2006): http://tinyurl.com/ya74o2z

[3] Timothy J. Dailey, *The Gathering Storm* (Tarrytown, NY: Revell, 1992), p. 157-158

[4] http://www.americanvision.org/the-american-vision-blog/pre-wrath-v-dispensationalism/

[5] Both John Hagee and Hal Lindsey quote nineteenth-century author John Cumming from his work, *The Destiny of Nations*. Cumming, in commenting on Russia's role in fulfilling Ezekiel's prophecy wrote, "This king of the North I conceive to be the autocrat of Russia...That Russia occupies a place, and a very momentous place, in the prophetic work has been admitted by almost all expositors." John Cumming, *The Destiny of Nations*, (London: Hurst & Blackette, 1864), n.p.; Quoted in Hal Lindsey, *The Late Great Planet Earth* (Grand Rapids, MI: Zondervan, 1970), p. 63

[6] Francis X. Gumerlock, *The Day and the Hour: Christianity's Perennial Fascination with Predicting the End of the World* (Powder Springs, GA: American Vision, 2000), p.26, 30

[7] ibid, p.42-44

[8] ibid, p.45

[9] ibid, p.47

[10] ibid, p.58

[11] ibid, p.84, 88

[12] ibid, p.114-116, 131,136-138

[13] Julius Kostlin, *Life of Luther* (New York, NY: Charles Scribner's Sons, 1893), p.400

[14] Mark U. Edwards Jr., *Luther's Last Battles: Politics and Polemics 1531-46* (Minneapolis, MN: Fortress Press, 1983), p.99

[15] ibid, p.99

[16] Thomas Newton, *Dissertation on the Prophecies Which Have Remarkably been Fulfilled at This Time Are Fulfilling in the World*, rev. ed. Rev. W. S. Dobson, (Philadelphia, PA: J. F. Dove, 1832), p.593

[17] Francis X. Gumerlock, *The Day and the Hour*, p.148, 161

[18] T.R., "Commentary on Ezekiel's Prophecy of Gog and Magog," *The Gentleman's Magazine* (October 1816), 307.

[19] ibid, p.306, 307

[20] Gary DeMar, "Hermeneutical Headlines", *American Vision* (October 30, 2006): http://www.americanvision.org/articlearchive/10-30-06.asp

[21] Matthew Henry, "Ezekiel", *Zondervan NIV Matthew Henry Commentary* (Grand Rapids, MI: HarperCollins Publishers Ltd., 1992) p.1106

[22] Clarke, Adam. "Commentary on Ezekiel 38". "The Adam Clarke Commentary". <http://www.studylight.org/com/acc/view.cgi?book=eze&chapter=038>. 1832.

[23] Robert Jamieson, A.R. Fausset, and David Brown, "Ezekiel" *Jamieson, Fausset, and Brown's Commentary on the Whole Bible* (Grand Rapids, MI: Zondervan, 1961), p.721

[24] William and Robert Chambers, *Chambers's Encyclopedia A Dictionary of Universal Knowledge*, 10 vols. London and Edinburgh (Philadelphia: J.B. Lippincott Company, 1888) 2:655

[25] Charles Taylor, *Calmet's Dictionary of the Holy Bible*, rev. ed. Edward Robinson (New York: Crocker and Brewster, 1832), p. 226

[26] Rev. T.K. Cheyne, J. Sutherland Black, *Encyclopaedia Biblica: A Critical Dictionary of the Literary Political and Religious History the Archeology Geography and Natural History of the Bible*, 4 vols. (London: Adam and Charles Black, 1903), 4:432

[27] Sverre Boe, *Gog and Magog: Ezekiel 38-39 as pre-text for Revelation 19, 17-21 and 20, 7-10* (Tubingen: Moher Siebeck, 2001), p. 92-97

[28] C.I. Scofield, *The Scofield Reference Bible* (New York: Oxford University Press, 1909)

[29] Hal Lindsey, *The Late Great Planet Earth* (Grand Rapids, MI: Zondervan, 1970)

[30] John Hagee, *Jerusalem Countdown: A Warning to the World* (Lake Mary, FL: Frontline 2006) also see Hagee's revised and updated version to this work; John Hagee, *Jerusalem Countdown: A Prelude to War* (Lake Mary, FL: Frontline, [2006], 2007)

[31] Joel Rosenberg, Epicenter: *Why The Current Rumblings In The Middle East Will Change Your Future* (Carol Stream, IL: Tyndale House, 2006)

[32] Mark Hitchcock, *The Coming Islamic Invasion of Israel,* (Sisters, OR: Multnomah Press, 2002)

[33] Mark Hitchcock, *Iran: The Coming Crisis-Radical Islam, Oil, and the Nuclear Threat* (Sisters, OR: Multnomah Press, 2006)

[34] John Cumming, *The End: The Proximate Signs Of The Close Of This Dispensation* (London: John Farquhar Shaw, 1855), p. 277

[35] John Cumming, *Redemption Draweth Nigh; The Great Preparation* (London: Richard Bentley, New Burlington Street, 1860), p.216

[36] Hal Lindsey, *The Late Great Planet Earth*, (Grand Rapids, MI: Zondervan, 1970), p.59

[37] ibid, p.67-70

[38] Hal Lindsey, *The 1980's: Countdown to Armageddon*, (New York, NY: Bantam Books, 1980), p.13

[39] ibid, p.63

[40] ibid, p.69

[41] Hal Lindsey, The Late Great Planet Earth, p.67

[42] Hal Lindsey, *Planet Earth–2000A.D.: Will Mankind Survive?* (Palos Verdes, CA: Western Front, 1994), 197. Of course, the implication is quite clear. If, as Hal Lindsey states, "The collapse of the Soviet state was absolutely necessary to the fulfillment of biblical prophecy" then why did he fail to

mention that in his first book *The Late Great Planet Earth* and again in *The 1980's: Countdown to Armageddon?* This is nothing but a total white wash and rewrite of what he has originally stated in the past. What is so sad is that people who continue to follow Hal Lindsey continue to give him a free pass and do not hold him accountable for his failed statements of the past.

[43] ibid, 200-201

[44] Gary DeMar, *Islam and Russia in Prophecy*, (Powder Springs, GA: American Vision, 2005), p.11

[45] The European Union welcomed ten new countries in 2004: Cyprus, the Czech Republic, Estonia, Hungary, Latvia, Lithuania, Malta, Poland, Slovakia and Slovenia. Bulgaria and Romania were admitted as members in 2007. Some of the countries listed above were either former Soviet Republics or former satellites of the former Soviet Union. (http://europa.eu/abc/european_countries/index_en.htm)

[46] "Bush: Follow Libya's Lead", *CBS News*, (December 20, 2003): http://www.cbsnews.com/stories/2003/12/22/world/main589735.shtml

[47] Scott Macleod, "Why Gaddafi's Now a Good Guy", *Time Magazine* (May 16, 2006): http://www.time.com/time/world/article/0,8599,1194766,00.html

[48] "US allows aircraft sales to Libya – official", *Reuters* (July 13, 2006): http://tinyurl.com/ybav8v6

[49] "Putin to Visit Israel In a Russian First", (March 23, 2005): http://www.newsmax.com/archives/articles/2005/3/22/222524.shtml

[50]"Putin Makes Historic Visit to Israel", (April 28, 2005): http://www.newsmax.com/archives/articles/2005/4/27/223025.shtml

[51] Hal Lindsey, "Persia's appointment with destiny", *WorldNetDaily,* (July 22, 2005): http://www.worldnetdaily.com/news/printer-friendly.asp?ARTICLE_ID=45396

[52] Hal Lindsey, "Iran, Russia and Ezekiel", (February 13, 2006): http://www.hallindseyoracle.com/articles.asp?ArticleID=12473

[53] ibid

[54] Dr. Dwight Wilson, *Armageddon Now! The Premillenarian Response to Russia and Israel Since 1917*(Tyler, TX: Institute for Christian Economics, [1977] 1991)

[55] Dr. Gary North, "Publisher's Preface", *Armageddon Now! The Premillenarian Response to Russia and Israel Since 1917*(Tyler, TX: Institute for Christian Economics, [1977] 1991), p. xvi

[56] ibid, p.xx

[56] On September 6, 2007, Israel launched a surprise air strike against what turned out to be a nuclear facility being built by Syria with the help of the North Korean government. According to an ABC report by Martha Raddatz, "the Israelis first discovered a suspected Syrian nuclear facility early in the summer, and the Mossad — Israel's intelligence agency — managed to either co-opt one of the facility's workers or to insert a spy posing as an employee" (Martha Raddatz, "EXCLUSIVE: The Case for Israel's Strike on Syria", http://abcnews.go.com/WN/Story?id=3752687). The cross border preemptive strike may also have been precipitated by the explosion of a Syrian Scud C missile that contained

VX and Sarin nerve agents killing 15 soldiers and wounding possibly 50 (Kenneth R. Timmerman, "Syrian Chemical Blast Preceded Israeli Strike", http://www.newsmax.com/timmerman/Syria_chem_blast/2007/09/21/34794.html). Needless to say, Israel's ability to strike deep into Syrian territory using non-stealth aircraft has Syria addressing the issue with Russia of how Israeli jets could have pulled this off without being detected using state of the art Russian anti-aircraft radar systems.

CHAPTER FOUR

Literal vs. Literally
(Literalistic)

—ɯ—

"Literal interpretation results in accepting the text of Scripture at its face value which involves recognizing distinctions in the Bible."[1]

~ Dictionary of Premillennial Theology

For those who believe that many of the Bible's prophecies await a future fulfillment (also known as futurism), claim that Bible prophecy should be interpreted literally. They believe that when it comes to biblical prophecy they take what the Bible has to say more literally than their non-futurist counterparts do. They emphatically state that they are guided by and follow the "Golden Rule of Biblical Interpretation": "When the plain sense of Scripture makes common sense, seek no other sense, but take every word at its primary, literal meaning, unless the facts of the immediate context clearly indicate otherwise."[2] According to Tim LaHaye, people who read the Bible like him "take Scripture literally whenever possible—unless some false teacher has clouded their thinking, rendering prophecy virtually impossible to understand by trying to interpret it through symbols or confusing allegories."[3] It is said that anyone interpreting the Bible in this particular way is said to be interpreting the Bible using a "literal" hermeneutic (*Hermeneutics* is the art and science of interpreting literature). Those who interpret the Bible in this fashion, claim that their principle of hermeneutics is that of literal interpretation. "This means interpretation that gives to every word the same meaning it would have in normal usage, whether employed in writing, speaking, or thinking."[4] Charles Ryrie in his book *Dispensationalism* wrote that the "Literal interpretation results in accepting the text of Scripture at its face value. Based on the philosophy that God originated language for the purpose of communicating His message to man and that He intended man to understand that message, literal interpretation seeks to interpret that message plainly." He also said that "If literal interpretation is the correct principle interpretation, it follows that it would be proper to expect it to apply to all the Scriptures."[5]

Contemporary Prophecy Writers Defending the Literal Hermeneutic

The author's of the book *The Truth Behind Left Behind* begin defending the "literal" interpretative methodology by using the dictionary to begin to define their approach to Biblical interpretation:

"The dictionary defines literal as "belonging to letters." It also says literal interpretation involve an approach "based on the actual words in their ordinary meaning...not going beyond the facts. The Oxford English Dictionary says, "Pertaining to the 'letter' (of Scripture); the distinctive epithet of that sense or interpretation (of the text) which is obtained by taking its words in their natural or customary meaning and applying the ordinary rules of grammar; opposed to *mystical, allegorical,* etc (emphasis in the original)."[6]

This interpretative methodology used by futurists like John Hagee, Hal Lindsey et al is also called the grammatical-historical method. According to the authors of *The Truth Behind Left Behind*, the grammatical component to the grammatical-historical interpretative method "considers the impact that grammar plays on a passage."[7] The historical component to the grammatical-historical interpretative method "means that the historical context must be taken into account. This aspect means that one must consider the historical setting and circumstances in which the books of the Bible were written."[8]

Prophecy teachers like Dr. Tim LaHaye and the authors of the book *The Truth Behind Left Behind* demand "that the Bible (including its prophetic portions) should be interpreted in the ordinary grammatical-historical way."[9] That is that the Bible "should be interpreted in its normative, literal sense, except in such instance where a figurative or nonliteral interpretation is obviously indicated."[10] Dr. Paul Lee Tan defines the literal approach this way: "To interpret "literally" means to explain the original sense of the speaker or writer according to the normal, customary, and proper usages of words and language. Literal interpretation of the Bible simply means to explain the original sense of the Bible according to the normal and customary usages of its language."[11]

For the futurist, the literal interpretation should be and "is to be the basic, primary way of approaching the texts of Bible prophecies."[12] When it comes to Biblical interpretation, those that adhere to the "Golden Rule of Biblical Interpretation" "approach the words of a Scripture passage in the same way that we would any other literature or any ordinary conversation."[13] As Ron Rhodes stated in his book *Northern Storm Rising*, "A literal interpretation of Scripture gives to each word in the text the same basic meaning it would have in normal, ordinary, customary usage whether employed in writing, speaking or thinking."[14]

Using the "Golden Rule of Biblical Interpretation" as opposed to an allegorical, metaphorical, or nonliteral interpretation, according to Tim LaHaye helps the interpreter to unlock passages that seem difficult to understand:

"The study of prophetic passages is not difficult when we take the Bible literally whenever possible. If, however, a person begins to spiritualize or allegorize the text, he is hopelessly doomed to confusion and error. Taking the Bible literally makes even difficult passages understandable."[15]

Therefore, the literal interpretation "looks to the text, the actual words and phrases of a passage. Allegorical or nonliteral interpretation imports an idea not found specifically in the text of a passage."[16]

Critics of this interpretative method have often claimed that this view often forces the interpreter into a rigid literalism also called "wooden literalism." Supporters of the "literal" method have countered the arguments of their critics by arguing that the grammatical-historical method "is a true and honest method"[17] of interpreting the Bible and does not discount the Bible's use of figures of speech.

Not only has this method been called "a true and honest method" it has also been called a "normal" and "plain" approach to interpreting Scripture. The theory goes that when the literal hermeneutic is applied to interpreting Scripture "every word written in Scripture is given the *normal* meaning it would have in its normal usage."[18] Charles Ryrie sums up this "normal" and "plain" approach stating, "The principle might also be called *normal* interpretation since the literal meaning of words is the normal approach to their understanding in all languages. It might also be designated *plain* interpretation so that no one receives the mistaken notion that the literal principle rules out figures of speech.

Symbols, figures of speech and types are all interpreted plainly in this method and they are in no way contrary to literal interpretation."[19]

For example, when Jesus calls himself the "true vine" in John 15 those that hold to the grammatical-historical method understand that Jesus is speaking figuratively. John Walvoord uses the exact scripture when making his case for the grammatical-historical method and its understanding of the uses figures of speech in the Bible:

"In the literal method, the words of Scripture are understood as indicated by the context in their ordinary, normal, customary, usage. This method recognizes that figurative language is frequently found in Scripture and that it always provides an understandable truth. Even though a figure is used, the passage teaches a literal truth. For example, Christ stated, "I am the true vine, and My Father is the vinedresser" (John 15:1). Throughout this figure, He spoke of people as branches and mentioned the fruit they bear. Christ was not literally a vine. However, the literal truth of the figure is clearly understandable."[20]

In his latest book on prophecy, a commentary on the book of Revelation titled *Because The Time Is Near*, respected theologian, Bible teacher, and author Dr. John MacArthur defends the "literal" interpretative methodology when he writes that only the "futurists approach provides justice to Revelation's claim as prophecy. Other approaches leave the meaning of Revelation to human opinion. The futurist approach takes the book's meaning as God gave it."[21] Or as Paul Benware put it: "Whenever we come to a prophetic passage, our commitment must be to understand that passage according to the accepted laws of language and not to seek some mystical figurative interpretation."[22]

Those that use and follow the "literal" method of biblical interpretation say that to leave this interpretative methodology is dangerous. "There has always been a great danger in leaving the grammatical-historical method of approaching the Bible" states Paul Benware, "because the interpreter who allegorizes the text essential becomes the final authority on the text's meaning."[23] Benware also stated, "when the literal interpretation of prophecy is abandoned, there is a lessened accountability to the text itself."[24] Therefore, according to this train of thought "If an interpreter does not use the normal, customary, literal method of interpreting Scripture, interpretation is given over to the unconstrained imagination of the interpreter."[25] Or as LaHaye put it "Once you begin heading down that road, however, everything is up for grabs. You can invent any kind of "interpretation" you want."[26]

Yet, in spite of these assertions of interpreting Biblical prophecy "literally," a review of these teachers' work on Biblical prophecy especially Ezekiel 38 and 39 will show an inconsistent literalism. One could even argue that it is a "choosy literalism." As you will see, when it comes to biblical prophecy, modern prophecy writers take a view that is less than literal in spite of their claims.

Telling Time

In his book on prophecy *Are We Living In The Last Days?*, respected Bible teacher and senior pastor of Harvest Christian Fellowship Church Greg Laurie wrote that he believed that the return of Jesus was going to take place soon. He believes that the movements toward a global economy, one-world religion, a one-world leader, and the isolation of Israel tell him "that Jesus is coming back very, very soon."[27] John Hagee echoed the same sentiments as Laurie in his 1996 book *Beginning of the End* under the heading Soon and Very Soon writing, "Messiah is soon to come. If you listen closely, you can hear the footsteps of Messiah walking through the clouds of heaven."[28] John MacArthur in his book *Because the Time is Near* comments "the book of Revelation deserves immediate proclamation because the end is near."[29] Taking these gentlemen's statements in a normal, ordinary, customary and literal way it is obvious that they are expecting the return of Jesus at the very least in their lifetime if not sooner; definitely not in the far distant future.

Compare their words to those of John in Revelation 1:1-3:

"The revelation of Jesus Christ, which God gave him to show his servants what must _soon_ take place. He made it known by sending his angel to his servant John, who testifies to everything he saw–that is, the word of God and the testimony of Jesus Christ. Blessed is the one who reads the words of this prophecy, and blessed are those who hear it and take to heart what is written in it because the time is _near_ (emphasis added)."

No matter when you believe the book of Revelation was written (pre-A.D. 70 or A.D. 95/96), there is little to no argument or disagreement that the book of Revelation was written in the first century to a first century audience. Of the events in Revelation, John said that they "must soon take place" (Rev 1:1) "because the time is near" (Rev 1:3). The same words and their equivalents are used in Revelation 3:11, 22:6, and 22:10. These two phrases open and close the book of Revelation and the point that John seems to be making to his reader's is the sense of urgency of the soon occurrence of his vision. Taken in a "plain," "primary," "common sense," "normative," and "literal" way why should soon, and near mean something other than what they seem to mean. Why should we take the words "soon" and "near" in Revelation 1:1-3 to mean something other than the way we use the words today?

In order to get around the force and obvious implications of John's statements, modern prophecy teachers, as the one's already mentioned, have re-interpreted these words and given them a much different meaning. These words have been reinterpreted as *"qualitative indicators* describing how Christ will return. How will He return? It will be "quickly" or suddenly.""[30] Thomas Ice, one of the preeminent modern prophecy futurist Bible teachers, agrees with his critics that the Greek word *tachos* can be translated shortly or soon.

However, he also claims that it can be translated to mean "quickly" or "suddenly." He has consistently cited Act 22:18 and 1 Timothy 3:14 as evidence to prove both possibilities. One particular critic of this approach has poignantly pointed out the inconsistency of this analysis:

"The problem with Ice's analysis is that "quickly" does not anticipate a delay in any of the verses where the word is used (e.g., Matt. 5:25; 28:7; Luke 15:22; 16:16; John 11:29, 31; 13:27; Acts 232:18). With "quickly", the action happens soon after. In fact, Ice uses Acts 22:18 as "descriptive of the manner in which the action takes place: 'I saw Him saying to me, "Make haste, and get out of Jerusalem *quickly*, because they will not accept your testimony about Me.""" If we apply Ice's understanding of "quickly" to this verse, it would read this way: "When you decide to get out of Jerusalem, do it *quickly*." But this makes no sense since Jesus' words were a warning to Paul to "make haste" in leaving the city, that is, to do it "quickly" because he had enemies in the city. If he waited and only acted speedily when he decided to leave, then Jesus' warning was inconsequential.

Ice contrasts Acts 22:18 with 1 Timothy 3:14, a verse he describes as a "timing passage": "I am writing these things to you, hoping to come to you *before long [en tachei]*." If 1 Timothy 3:14 is a timing passage, then so is Revelation 1:1 since both use the same Greek word (*en tachei*). The Greek construction is identical in all three verses (Acts 22:18; 1 Tim. 3:14; Rev. 1:1). So let's use "before long" in Revelation 1:1 and see how it reads: "The Revelation of Jesus Christ, which God gave Him to show to His bond-servant, the things which must take place *before long [en tachei]*." "Before Long" does not have the meaning of unspecified time going on for centuries!"[31]

Not to belabor the point but let's take a look at Matthew 24 verses 32 and 33. Modern prophecy teachers like the one's discussed in this chapter have always argued that the Olivet Discourse in Matthew's Gospel is dealing with a distressful period of time in the future called the Great Tribulation. In warning His disciples, Jesus used the fig tree He had just cursed (see Matthew 21:18-22) as an illustration. Toward the end of the Olivet Discourse, Jesus, after having answered the disciples question regarding His coming, used the parable of the fig tree to drive home a point. In Matthew 24:32-33 Jesus states,

"Now learn this lesson from the fig tree: As soon as its twigs get tender and its leaves come out, you know that summer is near. Even so, when you see all these things, you know that it[d]is near, right at the door."

John Walvoord who takes a much different view on this section of the Olivet Discourse than his futurist brethren, believes that a "better interpretation is that Christ was using a natural illustration"[32] instead of the fig tree representing national Israel. He stated that, "when those living in the great tribulation see the signs predicted, they will know that the second coming of Christ is near."[33]

Let's for one moment concede the point that dispensationalists are right and Jesus is speaking of a future great tribulation in the Olivet Discourse. If that is in fact the case, then why should those going through the Great Tribulation believe that Jesus return is near given the dispensational non-literal interpretation of the word *near*? How would that future generation know that the return of Jesus was near if near does not mean what it means in normal everyday speech? That is right around the corner, getting ready to happen, or "right at the door." When Jesus said, "As soon as its twigs get tender and its leaves come out, you know that summer is near" it is the same Greek word (*eggus*) that John used in Revelation 1:3. It would be incongruous, not to mention cruel, of John to be forewarning his first century audience about things that were to take place soon if the events were actually going to be taking place in the twenty-first century.

Every time near is used in the New Testament, it always means, "close" in terms of distance (Mark 2:2; Luke 15:1; John 11:18; Acts 1:12) or "close" in terms of time (Matt. 24:32; Luke 21:30). Shortly is used in a similar way (Act 25:4; Phil. 2:19, 24; 3 John 14).[34] As Gary DeMar has noted, "If literalism is the standard, there is no other way to interpret these time words."[35] As Milton Terry has stated, "When a writer says that an event will shortly and speedily come to pass, or is about to take place, it is contrary to all propriety to declare that his statements allow us to believe the event is in the far future. It is a reprehensible abuse of language to say that the words *immediately*, or *near at hand*, mean *ages hence*, or *after a long time*."[36]

Which Generation? "This" or "That"

Near, soon, and shortly are not the only time texts in which these prophecy teachers take a less than literal approach.

They also do the same with "this generation" in Matthew 24:34. Modern prophecy teachers have taught for some time now that the generation that saw Israel reborn as a nation in 1948 would be the generation that would see the Second Coming of Jesus. This view was built on the "belief that the "fig tree" illustration in verses 32-33 refers to the restored nationhood of Israel."[37] One such purveyor of this view is Hal Lindsey when he wrote in his bestseller *The Late Great Planet Earth*:

"When the Jewish people, after nearly 2,000 years of exile, under relentless persecution, became a nation again on 14 May 1948 the "fig tree" put forth its first leaves. Jesus said that this would indicate that He was "at the door," ready to return. Then He said, "Truly I say to you, *this generation* will not pass away until all this things take place" (Matthew 24:34 NASB).

What generation? Obviously, in context, the generation that would see the signs — chief among them the rebirth of Israel. A generation in the Bible is something like forty years. If this is a correct deduction, then within forty years or so of 1948, all these things could take place. Many scholars who have studied Bible prophecy all their lives believe that this is so."[38]

Other prophecy teachers have followed Lindsey's train of thought and have made similar statements using the fig tree illustration as proof.[39] Tim LaHaye has been just as emphatic as Hal Lindsey believing that the "this generation" of Matthew 24:34 "refers to those alive in 1948."[40] According to him, "That generation was old enough to "see" the United Nations officially recognize Israel as a nation."[41]

To his credit, LaHaye has accurately pinpointed the issue regarding Matthew 24:34, which is the meaning of "this generation." "The crucial issue concerns the meaning of "this generation"...In Greek, the demonstrative pronoun *haute* (this) always refers to the person or thing mentioned immediately before it." But he misses the mark when he continues by stating, "The thing mentioned just before "generation" involves those who see the sign of Israel as she either becomes a recognized nation or when she takes possession of most of Jerusalem."[42] Based on this non-literal interpretation by Lindsey and LaHaye of Matthew's use of "this generation" in 24:34, "this generation" has become "that generation."

The term "this generation" is used regularly in the Gospels and *without exception* it always applied to the contemporaries of Jesus. "Those who deny that "this generation" refers to the generation to whom Jesus was speaking in Matthew 24 context must maintain that "this generation" means something different from the way it is used in every other place in Matthew and the rest of the New Testament."[43]

The phrase "this generation" taken in a literal, normative and plain way is "a nonapocalyptic, nonpoetic, unambiguous, didactic assertion."[44] When you combine the Greek word for generation (*genea*) with the near demonstrative this (*haute*), there can only be one generation in mind; it is the generation to whom Jesus was talking too His contemporaries. "Without exception, the phrase "this generation" refers to the then present generation, not a generation that is "alive in 1948."[45]

- "To what can I compare *this generation?* They are like children sitting in the marketplaces and calling out to others..." (Matthew 11:16)

- "The men of Nineveh will stand up at the judgment with *this generation* and condemn it; for they repented at the preaching of Jonah, and now one greater than Jonah is here. The Queen of the South will rise at the judgment with *this generation* and condemn it..." (Matthew 12:41-42)

- "I tell you the truth, all this will come upon *this generation*." (Matthew 23:36)

- He sighed deeply and said, "Why does *this generation* ask for a miraculous sign? I tell you the truth, no sign will be given to it." (Mark 8:12)

- "If anyone is ashamed of me and my words in *this* adulterous and sinful *generation*, the Son of Man will be ashamed of him when he comes in his Father's glory with the holy angels." (Mark 8:38)

- "To what, then, can I compare the people of *this generation*? What are they like?" (Luke 7:31)

- As the crowds increased, Jesus said, "*This* is a wicked *generation*. It asks for a miraculous sign, but none will be given it except the sign of Jonah." (Luke 11:29)

- "For as Jonah was a sign to the Ninevites, so also will the Son of Man be to *this generation.*" (Luke 11:30)

- "The Queen of the South will rise at the judgment with the men of *this generation* and condemn them..."(Luke 11:31)

- "The men of Nineveh will stand up at the judgment with *this generation* and condemn it..."(Luke 11:32)

- "Therefore *this generation* will be held responsible for the blood of all the prophets that has been shed since the beginning of the world, from the blood of Abel to the blood of Zechariah, who was killed between the altar and the sanctuary. Yes, I tell you, *this generation* will be held responsible for it all." (Luke 11:50-51)

- With many other words he warned them; and he pleaded with them, "Save yourselves from *this* corrupt *generation.*" (Acts 2:40)

- "But first he must suffer many things and be rejected by *this generation.*" (Luke 17:25)

127

- "I tell you the truth, *this generation* will certainly not pass away until all these things have happened." (Matthew 24:34)

- "I tell you the truth, *this generation* will certainly not pass away until all these things have happened." (Mark 13:30)

- "I tell you the truth, *this generation*[b] will certainly not pass away until all these things have happened." (Luke 21:32)

A Horse is a Horse of Course and so are Swords, Shields and Arrows

Of course, these are not the only instances where a non-literal approach is taken. The same non-literal approach that is taken towards words "near", "soon", "shortly", and "this generation" is also applied to Ezekiel 38 and 39. As noted earlier, modern prophecy teachers, like those previously mentioned, demand that, the Bible in general and Bible prophecy specifically must be read in a literal fashion. These prophecy teachers claim that the literal approach "is to be the basic, primary way of approaching the texts of Bible prophecies." We have been told by these prophecy teachers that the literal method "gives to each word in the text the same basic meaning it would have in normal, ordinary, customary usage whether employed in writing, speaking or thinking."[46] When it comes to Ezekiel 38 and 39, however this approach to Biblical interpretation is totally and completely abandoned in favor of...you guessed it allegory and symbolism.

Gary DeMar has poignantly noted that "Any commentator writing prior to the invention of gunpowder could interpret Ezekiel's descriptive battle literally since wars were still fought with clubs, spears, and bows and arrows up until the eighteenth century. To account for an invasion that would use super-modern weapons such as jets and "atomic and explositve" devices, the battle of Gog and Magog must be interpreted symbolically, a methodology that LaHaye, at first reading, seems to reject. Those who see a symbolic battle claim that Ezekiel could describe distant future events only in terms that he and his readers understood."[47] The very same prophecy teachers that demand a literal approach to interpreting the Bible do a complete rewrite of this passage turning swords (38:4), shields (38:4; 39:9), spears (39:9), and bows and arrows (39:3, 9) into modern instruments of warfare.

For example, Mark Hitchcock and Thomas Ice state the following in their co-authored book *The Truth Behind Left Behind*: "Inspired by the Holy Spirit, Ezekiel spoke in language that the people of his day could understand. If he had spoken of MIG-29s, laser guided fired missiles, tanks, and assault rifles, this text would have been nonsensical to everyone until the twentieth century."[48] In justifying this interpretation, Mark Hitchcock has written, "Ezekiel, inspired by the Holy Spirit, spoke in language that the people of that day could understand. If he had spoken of planes, missiles, tanks, and rifles, this text would have been nonsensical to everyone until the twentieth century. This "modernizing" of the weapons is not spiritualizing the text but rather understanding God's word in its historical context in light of the original audience."[49]

Gary DeMar who has been one of the foremost critics of this interpretive methodology has called out these prophecy teachers on their interpretive inconsistency:

"What happened to the "golden rule of interpretation"? Why would the people in Ezekiel's day need to understand a prophecy if it wasn't meant for them? Why would the Holy Spirit confuse the people of Ezekiel's day and beyond for 2500 years and then confuse the generation it was meant for by describing a modern-day battle fought with ancient weapons?"[50]

Noting that Tim LaHaye has stated that the prophecies in Ezekiel 38 and 39 "are among the most specific and easy to understand in the prophetic world,"[51] he calls out LaHaye and those that follow his interpretive methodology with the following. "If this is true then why do LaHaye and others who follow his interpretive methodology force a less than literal interpretation on Ezekiel's two-chapter prophecy?"[52] He has also pointed out that if these prophecy teachers were to true their claim of literalism then there "should be a literal representation of the actual battle events as they are depicted in Ezekiel 38 and 39. There should be a one-to-one correspondence between Ezekiel's description of the battle and what they describe will take place."[53]

Tim LaHaye, Mark Hitchcock, Thomas Ice, et al are not the only ones that have drawn DeMar's ire for their interpretive inconsistency. So has Chuck Missler. Chuck Missler follows a similar approach to Ezekiel 38 and 39 as those already listed but takes the non-literal approach to the weapons in Ezekiel 38 and 39 a step further when he states in his book *The Magog Invasion* "the use of "horses (*soos*, or "leaper") may be simply idiomatic of motorized infantry." He continues with his non-literal interpretation by saying "These "bows and arrows' maybe more in the minds of the translators, speaking of 1611 A.D. technology. These terms could be regarded as synechdoches (terms where the specific is used to imply the general; or the general for the specific, etc.), such as (*keh-rev*), as for a destroying instrument, or "sword"... "Other examples could be (*khayts*), for a piercing missile: "arrow"; or (*keh-sheth*), for its associated launcher: a "bow." These terms could easily be idiomatic for "launchers" and "missiles.'"[54]

DeMar takes Chuck Missler to task for his non-literal interpretation approach to Ezekiel 38 and 39:

"To follow his interpretive methodology requires us to believe that the meaning of the Bible has been inaccessible to the people of God for nearly 2500 years...In order for Missler's interpretation to work, these things "must mean" what he claims so that the events described by Ezekiel have no application to his own day. Missler breaks all the rules of exegesis in his interpretation of Ezekiel 38 and 39...It is so counter to every principle of Bible interpretation ever developed."[55]

DeMar's criticism of these prophecy teachers and their inconsistent literalism has been so thorough and devastating, that it has lead one prophecy teacher in particular to agree with him. Thomas Ice has come to disagree with the statement he and coauthor Mark Hitchcock had made in *The Truth Behind Left Behind*: "Inspired by the Holy Spirit, Ezekiel spoke in language that the people of his day could understand. If he had spoken of MIG-29s, laser guided fired missiles, tanks, and assault rifles, this text would have been nonsensical to everyone until the twentieth century." Rather he has come to agree with Gary DeMar's sentiment that "A lot has to be read into the Bible in order to make Ezekiel 38 and 39 fit modern-day military realities that include jet planes, 'missiles,' and 'atomic and explosive' weaponry."[56] Ice further explains that:

"Since there does not appear to be demonstrable figures of speech or symbols in this passage for "army," "horses and horsemen," "buckler and shield," and "swords," then consistency requires that this battle will be fought with these items. These weapons of war cannot be similes for modern weapons since there are not textual indicators such as "like" or "as." There does not appear to be any figures of speech that sometimes occur without using a "like" or "as." For example, Jesus said, "I am the door," "I am the bread of life," etc. While these are not figures of speech in and of themselves, in their contexts it is clear that Jesus was speaking metaphorically. However, there is nothing in the context of Ezekiel 38, which would indicate that Ezekiel is seeing modern weapons yet using known terminology of his day.[57]

Even Mark Hitchcock is beginning to backtrack from the same statement he and Ice made in *The Truth Behind Left Behind*. Hitchcock, since the release of *The Truth Behind Left Behind* has consistently argued that the ""modernizing" of the weapons is not spiritualizing the text but rather understanding God's Word in its historical context in light of the original audience."[58] That is until now. Mark Hitchcock in a revision of John F. Walvoord's *Armageddon, Oil, and the Middle East Crisis* takes a more ambiguous view on how the weapons of Ezekiel 38 and 39 should be interpreted. The new revised edition titled *Armageddon, Oil, and Terror* states the following:

> "The burning of weapons (spears, bows, and arrows) for seven years has led some to wonder if the nations will regress to using primitive weapons in the end times. Others maintain that Ezekiel used ancient weapons that were familiar in his day to describe and anticipate modern weapons. We are not in a position today to settle this problem with any finality.

Whatever the explanation, the most sensible interpretation is that the passage refers to actual weapons pressed into use because of the peculiar circumstances of that day."[59]

Having read and re-read this section, I too have come to the same conclusion: that DeMar and Ice are absolutely correct. There is nothing in this text to suggest taking the war instruments in a non-literal way. "If we adhere strictly to the proper view of prophetic form, we must consider these weapons the same as that which will be used in eschatology. They must not be equated with vastly different modern war devices, as the H-bomb or the supersonic jet fighter."[60] Interpreted in a way that is "based on the actual words in their ordinary meaning...not going beyond the facts" a horse is a horse, a sword is a sword, and a shield is a shield. If we do then interpret Ezekiel 38 and 39 in a literal fashion were each word is taken "at its primary, literal meaning" then it leaves only one option.

"The battle in Ezekiel 38 and 39 is clearly an ancient one or at least one fought with ancient weapons. *All* the soldiers were riding horses (38:4, 15; 39:20). The horse soldiers were "wielding swords" (38:4), carrying "bows and arrows, war clubs and spears" (39:3, 9). The weapons were made of wood

(39:10), and the abandoned weapons served as fuel for seven years (39:9)."[61] With the overabundance of these weapons Israel would not have to gather wood from the fields or cut it from the forests (39:10), which obviously implies that the weapons are made from wood not titanium or any other alloyed material.[62]

"There is nothing in the context that would lead the reader to conclude that horses, war clubs, swords, bows and arrows, and spears mean anything other than horses, war clubs, swords, bows and arrows, and spears."[63] As DeMar has pointed out:

"If God wanted to picture a futuristic battle that included sophisticated and nearly impossible-to-describe weaponry, He could have used phrases such as "glowing metal" (Ezek. 1:4, 27), "burnished bronze" (1:7), "wings...spread out" (1:11, 23-24), "like burning coals of fire" (1:13), "like torches darting back and forth" (1:13), "like bolts of lightning" (1:14), "sparkling beryl" (1:16), "wheel within wheels" (1:16-17), "rising wheels" (1:19), "the gleam of crystal" (1:22), and "like the sound of an army camp" (1:24)."[64]

Literal (Literary) vs. Literally (Literalistic)

In spite of the claims by the aforementioned Bible prophecy teachers, it is obvious that they do not read the Bible in a literal fashion. A more apt description of their interpretive methodology would be literalistic (read wooden) rather than a literal interpretation. The issue at hand is what it means to interpret the Bible literally.

"When interpreting *any* literary work, we should always listen carefully to the author himself. Especially if he provides information affecting the proper approach to interpreting his work."[65] Interpreting the Bible literally or in a literal fashion "means that we are to interpret the Word of God just as we interpret other forms of communication—in the most obvious and natural sense."[66] Interpreting the Bible in a literally means the text should "be interpreted in the sense in which it is intended rather than in a literalistic sense."[67] For the students of Bible and Bible prophecy a proper "hermeneutic methodology becomes a paramount concern for the would-be interpreter."[68]

Hank Hanegraaf, also known as the Bible Answer Man, and theologian R.C. Sproul help define what it actually means to interpret the Bible literally as opposed to the overly simplistic definition given by Tim LaHaye. Hank Hanegraaff defines literal interpretation as the following:

> "To interpret the Bible literally, we must first pay special attention to what is known as *form* or *genre*. In other words, to interpret the Bible as literature, it is crucial to consider the kind of literature we are interpreting."[69]

R.C. Sproul in his book *Knowing Scripture* defines literal interpretation as the following:

> "The term *literal* comes from the Latin *litera* meaning letter. To interpret something literally is to pay attention to the *litera* or to the letters and words which are being used. To interpret the Bible literally is to interpret it as *literature*. That is, the natural meaning of a passage is to be interpreted according to the normal rules of grammar, speech, syntax and context...The principle of literal interpretation is a principle that calls for the closest kind of literary scrutiny of the text. To be accurate interpreters of the Bible we need to know the rules of grammar; and above all, we must be carefully involved in what is called *genre analysis*"[70]

R.C. Sproul continues on, writing, "The term genre means simply "kind", "sort", or "species." Genre analysis involves the study of such things as literary forms, figures of speech and style. We do this with all kind of literature. We distinguish between lyric poetry and legal briefs, between newspaper accounts of current event and epic poems. We distinguish between the style of historical narrative and sermons, between realistic graphic description and hyperbole. Failure to make these distinctions when dealing with the Bible can lead to a host of problems with interpretation. Literary analysis is crucial to accurate interpretation."[71]

As Hanegraaff has noted, "A literalistic method of interpretation often does as much violence to the text as does a spiritualized interpretation that empties the text of objective meaning. A literal-at-all-costs method of interpretation is particularly troublesome when it comes to books of the Bible in which visionary imagery is the governing genre."[72] Therefore, it is imperative that we as Bible interpreters interpret the Bible in a literary fashion as this will help prevent us from "imposing figurative meanings on passages not meant to be figurative."[73]

Notes

[1] Mal Couch and Joseph Chambers, "Literal Interpretation", *Dictionary of Premillennial Theology*, gen. ed Mal Couch (Grand Rapids, MI: Kregel Publications, 2004), p.95

[2] Tim LaHaye, *Understanding Bible Prophecy for Yourself* (Eugene, OR: Harvest House, 1998), p.14

[3] Tim LaHaye, "Introduction" in Mark Hitchcock and Thomas Ice, *The Truth Behind Left Behind: A Biblical View of the End Times* (Sisters OR: Multnomah Publishers, 2004), p.7

[4] Bernard Ramm, *Protestant Biblical Interpretation*, (Boston: W.A. Wilde, 1956), 89-92; Quoted in Charles C. Ryrie, *Dispensationalism* (Chicago: Moody, [1995], 2007), p.91

[5] Charles C. Ryrie, *Dispensationalism* (Chicago: Moody, [1995], 2007), p.102

[6] Mark Hitchcock and Thomas Ice, *The Truth Behind Left Behind: A Biblical View of the End Times* (Sisters OR: Multnomah Publishers, 2004), p.163

[7] ibid, p.167

[8] ibid, p.169

[9] Paul N. Benware, *Understanding End Times Prophecy: A Comprehensive Approach* (Chicago, IL: Moody Publishers, [1995] 2006), p. 98

[10] John F. Walvoord, *Israel In Prophecy* (Grand Rapids, MI: Zondervan, 1962) p.30

[11] Paul Lee Tan, *The Interpretation of Prophecy* (Rockville, MD: Assurance Publishers, 1974), p.29

[12] Paul N. Benware, Understanding End Times Prophecy, p.24

[13] ibid, p.23

[14] Ron Rhodes, Northern *Storm Rising: Russia, Iran, and the Emerging End-Times Military Coalition Against Israel* (Eugene, OR: Harvest House, 2007), p.95

[15] Tim LaHaye, *No Fear Of The Storm: Why Christians Will Escape All The Tribulation* (Sisters, OR: Multnomah, 1992), p.241

[16] Mark Hitchcock and Thomas Ice, *The Truth Behind Left Behind,* p.165

[17] Paul Lee Tan, *The Interpretation of Prophecy,* p.29

[18] Mal Couch, *An Introduction to Classical Evangelical Hermeneutics: A Guide to the History and Practice of Biblical Interpretation* (Grand Rapids, MI: Kregel Publications, 2000), p.33

[19] Charles C. Ryrie, *Dispensationalism,* p.91

[20] John F. Walvoord, *The Final Drama: 14 Keys to Understanding the Prophetic Scriptures* (Nashville, TN: Thomas Nelson, [1993], 1997), p.10

[21] John MacArthur, Because *The Time Is Near: John MacArthur Explains the Book of Revelation* (Chicago, IL: Moody Publishers, 2007), p.13

[22] Paul N. Benware, *Understanding End Times Prophecy,* p.24

[23] ibid, p.157

[24] ibid, p.27

[25] Mal Couch, *An Introduction to Classical Evangelical Hermeneutics*, p.36-37

[26] Tim LaHaye, "Introduction", *The Truth Behind Left Behind* ,p.7

[27] Greg Laurie, *Are We Living In The Last Days? How to be Prepared for the Lord's Return* (Dana Point, CA: Kerygma Publishing, 2005), p. 40

[28] John Hagee, *Beginning Of The End: The Assassination of Yitzhak Rabin and the Coming Antichrist* (Nashville, TN: Thomas Nelson, 1996), p.187

[29] John MacArthur, *Because The Time Is Near*, p.14

[30] Thomas Ice and Kenneth L. Gentry Jr., *The Great Tribulation: Past or Future? Two Evangelicals Debate the Question* (Grand Rapids, MI: Kregel Publications, 1999), p.107

[31] Gary DeMar, "When 'Near' Means 'Not Near' and 'Near' *Biblical Worldview Magazine* vol. 23 no.6 (June, 2007), p.6

[32] John F. Walvoord, *Matthew: Thy Kingdom Come: A Commentary on the First Gospel* (Chicago, IL: Moody, [1974] 1998), p.192

[33] ibid, p.192

[34] Gary DeMar, *End Times Fiction: A Biblical Consideration of the Left Behind Theology* (Nashville, TN: Thomas Nelson, 2001), p.56-57

[35] ibid, p.57

[36] Milton S. Terry, *Biblical Hermeneutics: A Treatise on the Interpretation of the Old and New Testaments* (reprint,

Grand Rapids, MI: Zondervan) p. 495-96; Quoted in Hank Hanegraaff, *The Apocalypse Code: Find Out What the Bible Really Says About the End Times...and Why it Matters* (Nashville TN: Thomas Nelson, 2007), p.160

[37] Gary DeMar, *Last Days Madness: Obsession of the Modern Church* 4th rev. ed. (Atlanta, GA: American Vision, 1999), p.178

[38] Hal Lindsey, *The Late Great Planet Earth* (Grand Rapids, MI: Zondervan, 1970), p.53-54

[39] Jack Kinsella, *The Last Generation: Ten Signs of the End of the Age* (Travelers Rest, SC: True Potential Publishing, 2007), p.32

[40] Tim LaHaye and Jerry Jenkins, *Are We Living in the End Times? Current Events Foretold in Scripture...and What They Mean* (Carol Stream, IL: Tyndale House Publishers, 1999), p.59

[41] ibid, p.59

[42] ibid, p.58

[43] Gary DeMar, *Last Days Madness*, p.56

[44] Thomas Ice and Kenneth L. Gentry Jr., *The Great Tribulation: Past or Future?*, p.28

[45] Hank Hanegraaff, *The Apocalypse Code: Find Out What the Bible Really Says About the End Times...and Why it Matters* (Nashville TN: Thomas Nelson, 2007), p.79

[46] Ron Rhodes, *Northern Storm Rising*, p.95

[47] Gary DeMar, *End Times Fiction*, p.11

[48] Mark Hitchcock and Thomas Ice, *The Truth Behind Left Behind,* p.47

[49] Mark Hitchcock, *Iran: The Coming Crisis-Radical Islam, Oil, and the Nuclear Threat* (Sisters, OR: Multnomah Press, 2006), p.186-187

[50] Gary DeMar, "Ezekiel's Magog Invasion: Future or Fulfilled?" *Biblical Worldview Magazine* vol. 22 no.12 (December, 2006), p.6

[51] Mark Hitchcock and Thomas Ice, *The Truth Behind Left Behind,* p.84

[52] Gary DeMar, "Ezekiel's Magog Invasion: Future or Fulfilled?", p.5

[53] ibid, p.4

[54] Chuck Missler, *The Magog Invasion* (Palos Verdes, CA: Western Front, 1995), p.174

[55] Gary DeMar, "Ezekiel's Magog Invasion: Future or Fulfilled?," p.5

[56] Thomas Ice, "Ezekiel 38 and 39: Part VIII." Ice quotes Gary DeMar in "Ezekiel's Magog Invasion: Future or Fulfilled?," p.4 http://www.pre-trib.org/article-view.php?id=321

[57] ibid

[58] Mark Hitchcock, "The Battle of Gog and Magog", http://www.pre-trib.org/article-view.php?id=257#_edn45

[59] John F. Walvoord with Mark Hitchcock, *Armageddon, Oil and Terror: What the Bible Says about the Future* 3rd rev. ed. (Carol Stream, IL: Tyndale House, 2007), p.99

[60] Paul Lee Tan, *The Interpretation of Prophecy*, p.223

[61] Gary DeMar, *End Times Fiction*, p.4

[62] Another reason to believe that the events of Ezekiel 38 &39 happened in the past is that Ezekiel 39:10 states, "They will not need to gather wood from the fields **or cut it from the forests**, because they will use the weapons for fuel." This verse seems to suggest that the climate in Israel was a lot more lush and green than it is today. There are other verses that suggest a much more lush and green climate existed in Israel than it does today which was teeming with lions, bears and wild boars (Joshua 17:14-16; Judges 14:5-9; 1 Samuel 17:33-37; 2 Samuel 17:8; 2 Samuel 18:5-9; 2 Samuel 18:16-18; 1 Kings 7:1-3; 1 Kings 13:23-28; 1 Kings 20:35-37; 2 Kings 2:23-24; 2 Kings 17:24-26; 2 Kings 19:22-24; Nehemiah 2:7-9; Jeremiah 5:5-7; Ezekiel 20:45-48). Again, a "literal" interpretation precludes this from happening sometime in the future, as there are no forests just as there are no lions or bears in Israel. Today Israel has a climate that is for the most part dry and arid. Essentially Israel is a desert paradise.

[63] Gary DeMar, *End Times Fiction*, p.4

[64] ibid, p.14-15

[65] Kenneth L. Gentry Jr., *The Book of Revelation Made Easy: You Can Understand Bible Prophecy* (Powder Springs, GA: American Vision Press, 2008), p.20

[66] Hank Hanegraaff, *The Apocalypse Code*, p.3

[67] ibid, p.10

[68] Kenneth L. GentryJr. , *The Book of Revelation Made Easy*, p.20

[69] Hank Hanegraaff, *The Apocalypse Code*, p.20

[70] R.C. Sproul, *Knowing Scripture* (Downers Grove, IL: InterVarsity Press, 1977), p.48-49

[71] ibid, p. 49

[72] Hank Hanegraaff, *The Apocalypse Code*, p.21

[73] R.C. Sproul, *Knowing Scripture*, p.56

CHAPTER FIVE

Is Modern Israel Fulfilling Prophecy?

—ɯ—

May 14, 1948 was a momentous day for the nation of Israel, for obvious reasons, as well as for many within the Christian community who believe that many of the Bible's prophecies that deal with Israel and the last days are still yet to be fulfilled. The return of Jews to Israel and the establishment of Israel as a nation in 1948 was seen as a fulfillment of Biblical prophecy. Now that Israel had been reestablished as a nation, God's prophetic time clock had been restarted and the countdown to the last days, the rapture of the Church, and the Second Coming of Christ was, and continues to be said were near, these events were going to happen soon, and to this generation. This would include the events outlined in Ezekiel 38 and 39. As one prominent prophecy writer stated, "The center of the entire prophetic forecast is the State of Israel. Certain events in that nation's recent history prove the accuracy of the prophets. They also force us to accept the fact that the "countdown" has begun... As Moses predicted, the Jewish nation was destroyed. And after nearly 2,000 years of wandering through exile, the Jews returned to Palestine and formed the nation of Israel on May 14, 1948. On that day, the prophetic countdown began!"[1]

The return of the Jews to the land of their forefathers was seen as vindication by many within the evangelical community of their end-time beliefs. Thomas Ice has summed up these sentiments:

"The arrival of the modern state of Israel on the world scene in 1948 was a big boon to the premillennial understanding of the Bible. This vindicates—in history—our biblical belief that God has a future plan for the land of Israel and the Jewish people. In spite of these developments, there are a group of evangelicals who think that the current state of Israel has nothing to do with God's biblical promises. How could anyone who claims to believe the Bible hold to such error? The current state of Israel is prophetically important because the Jewish people have been regathered in order to fulfill events during the coming seven-year tribulation period, following the rapture."[2]

Ezekiel chapter 37 is often used as a proof text to support the belief that the return of the Jews to Israel and the possession of the land by Jewish people today is a fulfillment of biblical prophecy. Even though this is one of many proof text used to support modern day Israel as being biblically significant it is the most often cited by many of today's popular prophecy writers. In Ezekiel 37:1-14, the prophet Ezekiel is given a vision of the restoration and return of the Jews back to the Promised Land symbolically pictured in a barren valley full of dead dry bones. This vision of the valley of dry bones is often stated to "represent the nation of Israel during the *Diaspora,* beginning in A.D. 70."[3] For example, Jack Kinsella, publisher and editor of the Omega Letter, in an article titled "The Amazing Accuracy of Ezekiel" wrote the following:

"Ezekiel wrote of Israel's regathering in the last days. In Ezekiel 37, the prophet is shown a valley of dry bones.

Those dry bones, the Lord explains, are the "whole house of Israel" (37:11) that the Lord says would be restored in the last days…The fulfillment of this prophecy could not be more obvious. The Jews of the Diaspora have indeed 'come from among the heathen' from 'every side' and returned to the Promised Land."[4]

"Many see Israel's return to the land as an integral part of Bible prophecy and consider its place on the world scene an essential part of the end times. This prophetic aspect was also one of the basic motivations of the Zionist movement itself. Jewish resurgence in the reborn State of Israel has a twofold significance: It confirms the accuracy of Scriptures, and it dramatically alerts the church to the sovereign activity of the Lord as He works in international affairs to fulfill his program."[5]

As Mark Hitchcock and Thomas Ice stated in their book *The Truth Behind Left Behind* "The gathering of the Jewish people to the land of Israel is an essential element in the Left Behind view of the end times. Just think about it. Almost every important event in this landmark series hinges on the existence of the nation of Israel."[6] This is a very accurate statement by Hitchcock and Ice. The gathering of the Jews to the land of Israel, as well as their continued existence in the land of Israel, is a foundational pillar in the prophetic worldview of Hitchcock and Ice and without it, this system cannot support itself. Not only is the return of the Jews seen as essential, but according to Ice, it is also seen as being biblically significant:

"Surely, anyone who claims to believe in a national future for Israel would have to say that the valley of dry bones prophecy in some way, shape, or form relates to modern Israel (Ezek.37:1-14). The prophet describes a future process through which the nation of Israel will come to be reconstituted and (when the process is complete) enter into a faithful spiritual relationship with the Lord. This multi stage process must surely include the current nation of Israel, in unbelief, that is being prepared to go through a time that will lead to her conversion to Jesus as their Messiah. This is said by Ezekiel to be a work of the Lord (Ezek. 37:14).Thus, the modern state of Israel is a work of God and biblically significant."[7]

The importance of the reestablishment of Israel is seen as a prophetic fulfillment of Ezekiel chapter 37 (the vision of the valley of dry bones) and in essence of God's covenant promise to Abraham found in Genesis 15:7-21 to give to him and his descendants the land of Israel. Now that the Jews are in the Promised Land, again it is often said that they are on the verge of fulfilling the land promises given to Abraham by God that many claim have never been fulfilled. With Israel now in the land and in the process of fulfilling the land grant promises as laid out in Genesis 15:7-21, we are now to believe that the end-times are upon us. This would include the invasion of Israel by Russia and her confederates, which is supposedly that much closer.

Stephen Sizer has done a good job of framing the issue of Israel's possession of the land around this one central question which is: "Does possession of the land by Jewish people today, and the existence of the State of Israel, have any theological significance in terms of the fulfillment of biblical prophecy within the purposes of God?"[8] It is an important question that should be answered by combing through the Bible in order to find the correct answer.

Divine Retribution for Dividing Israel

The contention by contemporary prophecy teachers that Israel has never attained the full allotment of land as promised by God is why there is such support for the nation of Israel to keep and expand its settlements in the West Bank and to leave Jerusalem as the undivided capital city of Israel. Any attempt to end the Israeli-Palestinian conflict via a two-state solution is met with swift condemnation. Any government or leader that gets involved to end the hostilities between the Israelis and Palestinians is considered as fighting against God's purposes for the nation of Israel and then becomes subject to the wrath of God and is therefore national and personal suicide.[15]

Pat Robertson went so far as to suggest this after then prime minister Ariel Sharon suffered a massive stroke on January 4, 2006. Robertson saw Ariel Sharon's stroke as divine retribution by God due to the dismantling of Jewish settlements in Gaza by Sharon. After Sharon suffered a debilitating stroke Robertson's response was, "He was dividing God's land and I would say, "Woe unto any prime minister of Israel who takes a similar course to appease the European Union, the United Nations or the United States of America. God says, 'This land belongs to me, and you'd better leave it alone.'"[16] Robertson also saw the assassination of Yitzhak Rabin as another instance of God's divine wrath by giving land to the Palestinians due to Rabin's signing of the Oslo Peace accords.[17] Michael Evans author of *The American Prophecies* has made similar statements regarding the United States. According to Evans, "If America divides Jerusalem, there will be no forgiveness. America will tragically end up on the ash heap of history."[18]

What Saith the Scriptures?

In spite of the claims of these prophecy experts, the overwhelming testimony of the Bible says something quite different. The Scriptures are very clear on whether or not the land promises to Israel have been fulfilled. There seems to be ample scriptural proof from the Bible that indicates that the promises made to Abraham by God regarding the Promised Land have been and were indeed fulfilled. The book of Joshua clearly indicates that the covenant promises to Abraham regarding the land were indeed fulfilled.

> **So Joshua took the entire land, just as the LORD had directed Moses, and he gave it as an inheritance to Israel according to their tribal divisions.** Then the land had rest from war. (Joshua 11:23; emphasis added)

> **So the LORD gave Israel all the land he had sworn to give their forefathers, and they took possession of it** and settled there.[44] The LORD gave them rest on every side, just as he had sworn to their forefathers. Not one of their enemies withstood them; the LORD handed all their enemies over to them.[45] **Not one of all the LORD's good promises to the house of Israel failed; every one was fulfilled.** (Joshua 21:43-45; emphasis added)

> Now I am about to go the way of all the earth. You know with all your heart and soul that **not one of all the good promises the LORD your God gave you has failed. Every promise has been fulfilled; not one has failed.**[15] But just as every good promise of the LORD your God has come true, so the LORD will bring on you all the evil he has threatened, until he has destroyed you from this good land he has given you. (Joshua 23:14-15; emphasis added)

The book of Nehemiah, written after the Babylonian exile, testified to the fulfillment of God's promises to Abraham. Upon the return from exile, the nation of Israel gathered together in the presence of God where they read from the Book of the Law and confessed their sins. It is during this national day of penance that the book of Nehemiah states the crowd's recognition of the fulfillment of the covenant made to Abraham.

> "You are the LORD God, who chose Abram and brought him out of Ur of the Chaldeans and named him Abraham.[8] You found his heart faithful to you, and **you made a covenant with him to give to his descendants the land of the Canaanites, Hittites, Amorites, Perizzites, Jebusites and Girgashites. You have kept your promise** because you are righteous." (Nehemiah 9:7-8; cf. Genesis 15:18-21, emphasis added)

> "You gave them kingdoms and nations, allotting to them even the remotest frontiers. They took over the country of Sihon king of Heshbon and the country of Og king of Bashan. [23] **You made their sons as numerous as the stars in the sky, and you brought them into the land that you**

told their fathers to enter and possess.[24] **Their sons went in and took possession of the land.** You subdued before them the Canaanites, who lived in the land; you handed the Canaanites over to them, along with their kings and the peoples of the land, to deal with them as they pleased.[25] They captured fortified cities and fertile land; they took possession of houses filled with all kinds of good things, wells already dug, vineyards, olive groves and fruit trees in abundance. They ate to the full and were well-nourished; they reveled in your great goodness. (Nehemiah 9:22-25; cf. Genesis 15:5; 13:16; 22:17; Deuteronomy 6:10-11; 8:7-10, emphasis added)

The prophet Jeremiah echoes the statements of Nehemiah in a prayer to the Lord saying:

You brought your people Israel out of Egypt with signs and wonders, by a mighty hand and an outstretched arm and with great terror.[22] **You gave them this land you had sworn to give their forefathers**, a land flowing with milk and honey.[23] **They came in and took possession of it**, but they did not obey you or follow your law; they did not do what

157

you commanded them to do. So you brought all this disaster upon them. (Jeremiah 32:21-23; emphasis added)

Notice that the aforementioned scriptures state that the Israelites "took possession of the land" and not part of the land. Even the biblical books of Kings and Chronicles state that the promises God made to Abraham were indeed fulfilled and they go on to state that the nation of Israel reached the borders that God had previously promised to Abraham:

The people of Judah and Israel were as numerous as the sand on the seashore; they ate, they drank and they were happy.[21] **And Solomon ruled over all the kingdoms from the River** [b] **to the land of the Philistines, as far as the border of Egypt.** These countries brought tribute and were Solomon's subjects all his life...For he ruled over all the kingdoms west of the River, from Tiphsah to Gaza, and had peace on all sides.[25] During Solomon's lifetime Judah and Israel, from Dan to Beersheba, lived in safety, each man under his own vine and fig tree. (1 Kings 4:20-21; 24-25; emphasis added)

Praise be to the LORD, who has given rest to his people Israel just as he promised. Not one word has failed of all the good promises he gave through his servant Moses. (1 Kings 8:56; emphasis added)

Moreover, David fought Hadadezer king of Zobah, as far as Hamath, when **he went to establish his control along the Euphrates River.** (1 Chronicles 18:3)

So Solomon observed the festival at that time for seven days, and **all Israel with him—a vast assembly, people from Lebo Hamath to the Wadi of Egypt.** (2 Chronicles 7:8)

He [Solomon] ruled over all the kings **from the River to the land of the Philistines, as far as the border of Egypt.** (2 Chronicles 9:26)

As Gary DeMar has pointed out, "All the elements necessary for the fulfillment of the Abrahamic covenant as related to the land are present in these verses: God gave the Israelites the land He had promised to give; they possessed and lived in the land; they had rest; their enemies did not stand before them; not one of the promises God made to the house of

Israel failed. If these verses do not teach what they seem to teach, then how else could God have put it, said it, or written it if He had *wanted* to inform the Israelites that they had in fact possessed the land as promised?"[19]

As you can see in spite of the claims that Israel never fully possessed the land the evidence from the Bible is very clear. The Bible is very clear that the nation of Israel did indeed reach the boundary limits God had promised in Genesis chapter 15. The kingdom of Israel reached the height of its existence and included the most territory under the reign of King David (1000–961 BC). Its borders stretched far beyond present-day Israeli borders and included parts of what is now Lebanon, Syria, Jordan, and Egypt.[20]

Land Promises: Fulfilled or Unfulfilled?

Paul Boyer has pointed out in his book *When Time Shall Be No More* Israel's expansion to its biblical borders has become an article of faith for today's popular prophecy writers.[9] Using Tim LaHaye as an example of this kind of thought, Boyer pointed out how LaHaye "in 1984 illustrating his point that "the Jews of today occupy only a small portion of what God intended for them to enjoy," superimposed "God's Original Land Grant to Israel" on a map of the modern Middle East; it showed Israel absorbing all of Lebanon, part of Saudi Arabia, and most of Jordan, Syria, and Iraq."[10]

In Genesis 15:7-21 God promised to give the land of Israel to Abraham and his descendants as an inheritance. In these verses, God gives the boundaries of the Promised Land to be from the river of Egypt (Wadi el-Arish) to the Euphrates River.

On that day the LORD made a covenant with Abram and said, "To your descendants I give this land, from the river of Egypt to the great river, the Euphrates- the land of the Kenites, Kenizzites, Kadmonites, Hittites, Perizzites, Rephaites, Amorites, Canaanites, Girgashites and Jebusites." (Genesis 15:18-21)

It is often claimed that this promise was never fulfilled by Israel. There are those that contend that since Israel never fully possessed the land in its totality as outlined in Genesis 15 this promise by God is yet to be fulfilled. For example, Tim LaHaye has stated, "[W]e believe that God must fulfill to Israel as a national entity those promises made through unconditional covenants like the Abrahamic, Davidic, and Land of Israel. If this is true, then they must be fulfilled literally, and that means many aspects are yet future."[11] J. Dwight Pentecost and John Walvoord are even more dogmatic in their belief that Israel's land grant promises have never been fulfilled. They emphatically assert in their co-authored book *Things to Come: A Study in Biblical Eschatology,* "Suffice it to say at the present that Israel's history, even under the glories of the Davidic and Solomonic reigns, never fulfilled that promised originally to Abraham."[12] It is argued that this will only happen when Jesus returns. This is also the same argument taken up by Ron Rhodes. In his book *Northern Storm Rising* he contends, "[e]eventually, Israel will finally and wonderfully come to recognize Jesus as the divine Messiah and come into full possession of the promised land. The fullness of this possession will be in the future millennial kingdom."[13] Allen Ross of the Dallas Theological Seminary made a similar statement in *The Bible Knowledge Commentary* writing, "Israel has never possessed this land in its entirety, but she will when Christ returns to reign as Messiah"[14]

Unconditional or Conditional

In chapter seventeen of Genesis, God confirms the covenant that He had made with Abraham in chapter fifteen establishing it as an everlasting covenant (Genesis 17:7-8, 13, 19). Since it is called an everlasting covenant by God it is often seen as unconditional and since it is therefore "unconditional" the Jewish claims to the land continue in perpetuity. Based on the unconditional nature of the land promises, the Jews therefore have a permanent and perpetual claim to the land. But that is the crux of the issue. Are the promises regarding the land truly "unconditional" or were they in fact conditional?

In Genesis 17:7-8, 13, 19 when God told Abraham that He was establishing an everlasting covenant with Abraham it is taught that this everlasting covenant was an unconditional covenant. Since the Bible describes the Abrahamic covenants as everlasting then it must surely mean "eternal" or "lasting and enduring for all time." For example, J. Dwight Pentecost has written that the covenant that God made with Abraham "according to the Scriptures, are *eternal*."[21] Since aspects of this covenant are eternal it therefore guarantees "Israel a permanent national existence, perpetual title to the land, and the certainty of material and spiritual blessing through Christ"[22] in spite of the fact that they are not adhering to the dictates of the covenant.

Paul Benware echoed a similar line of thought in his book *Understanding End Times Prophecy* writing, "He [Abraham] was told that God would prosper him and give him the land of Canaan for an everlasting possession. The blessings given to Abraham's descendants (the *national* blessings) would come through Isaac and Jacob. Those blessings included the guarantee of national existence as well as the greatness of the nation, the land area of Canaan as an everlasting possession, and the continuation of the Abrahamic covenant as an everlasting covenant...The everlasting nature of the Abrahamic covenant means that the nation of Israel must exist forever as a nation in relationship with God."[23]

Jewish possession of the land was always contingent on their covenantal obedience. One needs to go no further than Genesis 17. In Genesis 17 God, after confirming his covenant with Abraham (vv. 2-8), commanded that Abraham and his descendants after him obey the covenant by circumcision. Failure to keep this commandment would result in the uncircumcised being cut off from his people (land). "Those who rejected circumcision rejected the sign of the covenant. They were no friends of the covenant God made with Abraham. It wasn't that circumcision made them a part of the covenant (faith did), but rejection of circumcision was a rejection of the covenant."[24]

Joshua in his farewell address to the Israelites forewarned them that God would expel them from the land if they transgressed his laws:

"**But just as every good promise of the LORD your God has come true,** so the LORD will bring on you all the evil he has threatened, until he has destroyed you from this good land he has given you.[16] **If you violate the covenant of the LORD your God,** which he commanded you, and go and serve other gods and bow down to them, the LORD's anger will burn against you, and **you will quickly perish from the good land he has given you**"(Joshua 23:15-16).

It is obvious from the reading of these verses that possession of the land was conditional to Israel being obedient to and not violating the covenant. The warning given by Joshua echoes the same warning that Moses gave to the very same generation of Israelites, as they were getting ready to possess the land:

"See, I set before you today life and prosperity, death and destruction.[16] For **I command you today to love the LORD your God, to walk in his ways, and to keep his commands, decrees and laws**; then you will live and increase, and the LORD your God will bless you in the land you are entering to possess. [17]But if your heart turns away and you are not obedient, and if you are drawn away to bow down to other gods and worship them,[18] I declare to you this day that you will certainly be destroyed. You will not live long in the land you are crossing the Jordan to enter and possess" (Deuteronomy 30:15-18).

Here again obedience to the covenant is a condition of continued possession of the land that God had promised to the Israelites.

Everlasting or Everlasting

The other issue surrounding the land promises and its fulfill-ment is really around how the word everlasting should be understood. For those that see the land promises as yet to be fulfilled believe that the word *olam* should be interpreted in literal fashion. On this issue, John Walvoord writes:

"The Hebrew expression for "everlasting" is *olam*, meaning "in perpetuity." While it might not quite be the equivalent of the infinite term "everlasting," it would certainly mean continuance as long as this present earth should last. It is the strongest expression for eternity of which the Hebrew language is capable."[25]

The best determiner of how a word in the Bible should be understood is the Bible itself instead of some arcane definition that is ambiguous at best. The word *olam* is used many times in the Old Testament and is used in conjunction with many things that does not fit the definition as laid out by Walvoord. For example, in Genesis God told Abraham that circumcision of the flesh, a sign of the covenant, was to be done as an everlasting covenant:

> Then God said to Abraham, "As for you, you must keep my covenant, you and your descendants after you for the generations to come.[10] This is my covenant with you and your descendants after you, the covenant you are to keep: Every male among you shall be circumcised.[11] You are to undergo circumcision, and it will be the sign of the covenant between me and you.[12] For the generations to come every male among you who is eight days old must be circumcised, including those born in your household or bought with money from a foreigner—those who are not your offspring.[13] Whether born in your household or bought with your money, they must be circumcised. My covenant in your flesh is to be an ever-lasting (*olam*) covenant.[14] Any uncircumcised male, who has not been circumcised in the flesh, will be cut off from his people; he has broken my covenant." (Genesis 17:9-14)

In the Old Testament, the name Jew and the rite of circumcision were outward symbols of separation from the pagan and heathen cultures and a sign of devotion and obedience to the God of salvation.[26] In Romans, Paul discusses the rite of circumcision as practiced in the Old Testament and puts it in its proper perspective in light of the New Testament. According to Paul, true circumcision "is not that which is outward in the flesh and in the letter." Rather true circumcision "is that which is inward, of the heart, and in the spirit. It is the heart that God looks at, the circumcising of the heart that renders us acceptable to him (see Deuteronomy 30:6)."[27] The editors of the *NIV Study Bible* noted that "The true sign of belonging to God is not an outward mark on the physical body, but the regenerating power of the Holy Spirit within."[28] The physical aspect of circumcision practiced in the Old Testament was a type and shadow of which the New Testament reality is the fulfillment.

In Exodus, the Aaronic priesthood is said to be an everlasting priesthood before the Lord: "You shall anoint them, as you anointed their father, that they may minister to Me as priests; for their anointing shall surely be an everlasting (*olam*) priesthood throughout their generations" (Exodus 40:15 KJV). In Leviticus, God said that the statute regarding the Day of Atonement was to be everlasting: "And this shall be an everlasting (*olam*) statute unto you, to make an atonement for the children of Israel for all their sins once a year. And he did as the LORD commanded Moses" (Leviticus 16:34 KJV). Again, in Leviticus the twelve loaves of bread that was to be set before the Lord regularly on the Sabbath in the Tabernacle was to be done so as an everlasting covenant: "And thou shalt put pure frankincense upon each row, that it may be on the bread for a memorial, even an offering made by fire unto the LORD. Every sabbath he shall set it in order before the LORD continually, being taken from the children of Israel by an everlasting (*olam*) covenant" (Leviticus 24:7-8 KJV). Phineas the son of Eleazar was promised an everlasting priesthood by God for his zealous act in the book of Numbers: "And he shall have it, and his seed after him, even the covenant of an everlasting (*olam*) priesthood; because he was zealous for his God, and made an atonement for the children of Israel" (Numbers 25:13 KJV). The Levititcal and Aaronic priesthoods, the tabernacle, the Temple and Temple service have been superseded by Christ's finished work on the cross and the New Covenant (see Hebrews 7; 8; 9;10; cf. Galatians 4:21-31). These were types and shadows that pointed to the ultimate reality in which they find their everlasting fulfillment (see Colossians 2:17; Hebrews 8:1-6; 10:1; cf. Exodus 25:40). So it is with the land.

"In his letter to a predominantly Gentile church in Ephesus Paul applies the promise of the inheritance of the land specifically to Gentile children of Christian believers who are obedient.

"Children, obey your parents in the Lord, for this is right." Honor your father and mother"—which is the first commandment with a promise "that it may go well with you and that you may enjoy long life on the earth." (Ephesians 6:1-3)

The fifth commandment promised that obedient children would live long on the land the Lord God was giving them. Now Paul applies the same promise to the children of Christian parents living 700-800 miles from the land of the Bible. These children of Gentile and Jewish Christians who submit willingly to the authority of their parents will, Paul promises, enjoy long life on the earth. Land in the New Covenant context has now come to fulfillment in the purposes of God. The limitations of the land type under the Old Covenant has been broken so that it stretches as far as the Great Commission to the uttermost ends of the earth."[29]

Therefore, it is "Under the Old Covenant, revelation from God came in shadow, image, form and prophecy. In the New Covenant, we have reality, substance and fulfillment. The question is not whether the promises of the covenant are to be understood literally or spiritually. It is instead a question of whether they should be understood in terms of Old Covenant shadow or in terms of New Covenant reality. The same principle applies to the promises concerning the Land which are also serving as revelational shadows, images, types, prophecies, anticipating God's future purposes, not only for one small people the Jews, but the whole world, revealed fully and finally in Jesus Christ...Once this consummation has been reached, never again would the revelation from God suggest that his people should aspire to the paradigms of the Old Covenant. Retrogression to the older shadowy forms of the Old Covenant were forbidden. God's children have become temples in which His shekinah glory dwells. To suggest therefore that the shekinah is to return to a single local geographical shrine to which we must come to worship is to regress from the reality to the shadowy, to re-erect the dividing curtain of the Temple, to apostasize from the New to the Old Covenant, because it is to impugn the atoning work of Christ."[30]

Notes

[1] Hal Lindsey, *The 1980's: Countdown to Armageddon* (New York, NY: Bantam Books, 1980), p.11-12

[2] http://www.pre-trib.org/article-view.php?id=110

[3] John Hagee, *Jerusalem Countdown: A Warning to the World* (Lake Mary, FL: Frontline, 2006), p.94-95

[4] http://www.omegaletter.com/articles/articles.asp?ArticleID =2372&SearchFor=lost_-_tribes_-_of_-_Israel

[5] Stanley A. Ellise and Charles H. Dyer, *Who Owns The Land?: The Arab-Israeli Conflict* (Carol Stream, IL:Tyndale House Publishers, 2003), p.114

[6] Mark Hitchcock and Thomas Ice, *The Truth Behind Left Behind: A Biblical View of the End Times* (Sisters OR: Multnomah Publishers, 2004), p. 57

[7] http://www.pre-trib.org/article-view.php?id=40

[8] http://www.cc-vw.org/articles/debate.html

[9] Tim LaHaye and Thomas Ice, *Charting the End Times* (Eugene, OR: Harvest House, 2001), p.78

[10] J. Dwight Pentecost and John F. Walvoord, *Things to Come: A Study in Biblical Eschatology* (Grand Rapids, MI: Zondervan, [1958] 1964), p.82

[11] Ron Rhodes, *Northern Storm Rising: Russia, Iran, and the Emerging End-Times Military Coalition Against Israel* (Eugene, OR: Harvest House, 2007), p.75

[12] Allen P. Ross, "Genesis", *The Bible Knowledge Commentary: Old Testament*, eds. John F. Walvoord and Roy B. Zuck (David C. Cook, 1985), p.56. ©1985 Cook Communications Ministries. *Bible Knowledge Commentary: Old Testament* by Walvoord and Zuck. Used with permission. May not be further reproduced. All rights reserved.

[13] Paul Boyer, *When Time Shall Be No More Israel's: Prophecy Belief In Modern American Culture* (Cambridge, MA: Harvard University Press, 1994), p.194

[14] ibid, p.195

[15] Joel 3:1-2 is often used by today's prophecy teachers and writers as a warning against any proposed peace initiative that involves Israel giving up land to the Palestinians. Joel 3:1-2 states, "I will enter into judgment with them there on behalf of my people and my inheritance, Israel, whom they have scattered among the nations; and they have divided up my land." This was the contention of John Hagee in his book *Jerusalem Countdown*: "The Roadmap for Peace is an ill-conceived document, one that has Israel giving up Gaza, then the West Bank, and then Jerusalem. It clearly violates the Word of God. How so? Joel 3:2 says, "I will also gather all nations [this includes America], and bring them down to the Valley of Jehoshaphat; and I will enter into judgment with them there on account of My people, My heritage Israel… they have divided my land." When America forced Israel to give up Gaza, it was clearly violating Joel 3:2." John Hagee, *Jerusalem Countdown: A Warning to the World* (Lake Mary, FL: Front Line, 2006), p.25. As proof to support the contention that dividing the land of Israel is against the will of God they point to the natural disasters that have hit the United States. For example, Jennifer James argues that the 375 tornadoes that ripped across the U.S. heartland in May 2003 was a direct result of U.S. Consul General Jeffrey Feltman

comments on implementing a two state solution. James is not alone in echoing these sentiments. Bill Koenig has stated very similar thoughts in his book *Israel: The Blessing Or the Curse* of which James quotes extensively in her article. Jennifer James, "Acts of God: America's Warning Not to Divide Israel,": (http://www.soundanalarm.net/DividingIsr aelsCovenantLand.html)   http://www.cbn.com/CBNNews/ News/030626a.asp;. The prophecy of Joel has nothing to do with today's geopolitical setting in the Middle East. The fortunes of Judah and Jerusalem were restored with the return of the exiles from Babylonian exile (see the books of Ezra and Nehemiah). Therefore, the nations that were to be judged by God were nations that were responsible for sending them into slavery in the first place (Joel 3:3-8).

[16] http://www.metimes.com/International/2006/01/09/ robertson_suggests_sharon_smote_by_god/1022/

[17] http://www.foxnews.com/story/0,2933,180774,00.html

[18] Michael D. Evans, *The American Prophecies: Ancient Scriptures Reveal Our Nation's Future* (New York, NY: Warner Faith, 2004), p.27

[19] Gary DeMar, "Is Israel's Land Prophetically Significant?" *American Vision* (September 30, 2005): http://web. archive.org/web/20060301032756/www.americanvision. org/articlearchive/09-30-05.asp

[20] http://encarta.msn.com/media_461532970/kingdom_of_ israel.html

[21] J. Dwight Pentecost, *Things to Come: A Study in Biblical Eschatology*, p.69

[22] ibid, p.71

[23] Paul N. Benware, *Understanding End Times Prophecy: A Comprehensive Approach* (Chicago: Moody Press, [1995] 2006), p.37, 49

[24] Guzik, David. "Study Guide for Genesis 17." Enduring Word. Blue Letter Bible. 7 Jul 2006. 2009. 20 Jun 2009 http://www.blueletterbible.org/commentaries/comm_view. cfm?AuthorID=2&contentID=7337&commInfo=31&topic =Genesis

[25] John F. Walvoord, *Israel In Prophecy* (Grand Rapids, MI: Zondervan, 1962), p.48

[26] Jamieson, Robert, A.R. Fausset, and David Brown, "Romans" *Jamieson, Fausset, and Brown's Commentary on the Whole Bible* (Grand Rapids, MI: Zondervan, 1961), p.1144

[27] Matthew Henry, "Romans," *Zondervan NIV Matthew Henry Commentary* (Grand Rapids, MI: HarperCollins Publishers Ltd., 1992), p.568

[28] *Zondervan NIV Study Bible*, "Romans," ed. Kenneth L. Barker (Grand Rapids, MI: Zondervan, 2002), p.1742

[29] http://www.cc-vw.org/articles/debate.html

[30] ibid

CHAPTER SIX

Identifying Rosh and the Gang

—ɯ—

Russia, since the nineteenth century and all throughout the twentieth century, has been the leading candidate to fulfill the role of Gog in Ezekiel 38-39. During this period, Russia's role in prophecy has been claimed to be a near certainty amongst those that have constantly commented and wrote bestselling books on the prophetic portions of Scripture. For example, writing in 1907 Arno C. Gaebelein wrote in his book *The Harmony of the Prophetic Word* "as we have seen in the other passages, a confederacy of nations is accomplished before the day of Jehovah, and these nations come down upon the land. That the land of the north and the immense territory acquired by that land—we mean Russia—will be in that confederacy is obvious."[1]

Modern prophecy writers have picked up on and opined similar thoughts as their brethren from the past. For instance John F. Walvoord considered by many to be the father of modern day prophetic thought stated, "Today, to the north of the nation Israel is the armed might of Russia. Never before has it seemed more likely that the prediction will be fulfilled given by Ezekiel (chapter 38-39) of an invasion from the north."[2] The twentieth century is replete with books and articles assuring readers that Russia is *clearly* mentioned in the Bible. "Nearly every modern-day prophecy book comes to the same conclusion. Russia is Ezekiel's "Gog," with its leader being the "prince of Rosh.""[3]

Rosh, Russia, and Etymology

Initially, the idea that Russia was the end-times bad-guy being prophesied by Ezekiel in chapters 38 and 39 was in part due to the similarity in sound of the Hebrew words *rosh*, Meshech and Tubal with Russia and its cities Moscow and Tobolsk. For instance, "Tim LaHaye claims to know that Ezekiel 38 and 39 "can only mean modern-day Russia" because of "etymology," that is, by studying the origin of words."[4] LaHaye has claimed, "Etymologically, the Gog and Magog of Ezekiel 38 and 39 can only mean modern-day Russia."[5]

"Here is how it works. In Ezekiel 38:2 and 39:1, the Hebrew word *rosh* is translated as if it were the name of a nation. That nation is thought to be modern Russia because *rosh* sounds like Russia. In addition, *Meschech* (38:2) is said to sound like Moscow, and *Tubal* (38:2) is similar to the name of one of the prominent Asiatic provinces of Russia, the province of Tobolsk."[6] This is exactly what Tim LaHaye does in his book *The Beginning Of The End* where he states, "The name Moscow comes from the tribal name Meshech, and Tobolsk, the name of the principal state, comes from Tubal. The noun Gog is from the original tribal name, Magog, which gradually became "Rosh", then "Rus" and today is known as Russia."[7]

The *rosh* as Russia connection can in part be traced back to the Hebrew lexicographer Wilhelm Gesenius. "Heinrich Friedrich Wilhelm Gesenius (1786-1842) was a Hebrew lexicographer and professor of theology of extraordinary ability at the University of Halle in Prussia. His most noted work is the Hebrew and Chaldee Lexicon, the first part of which was published in 1829."[8] Gesenius's influence as a master of Hebrew is widespread. The editors of the Brown-Driver-Briggs lexicon refer to him as the father of modern Hebrew lexicography.[9] In his lexicon, Gesenius identifies Rosh as "a northern nation mentioned along with Tubal and Meshech" which he specifically claims is *"the Russians."*[10] So influential was his work that many prophecy writers have followed the template laid down by Gesenius. Writers that subscribe to the *rosh*=Russia connection have often appealed to him for support. Gesenius, thus, has become one of the foundational pillars to the *rosh*=Russia connection.[11] You can see the impact that Gesenius had by reading the works of prophecy writers writing right after the publishing of Gesenius' lexicon.

For example, John Gaylord in a prophecy related work released in 1855, believed that the *rosh*/Russian connection was credible, writing, "that from the Rosh and Meshech are descended the Russians and Muscovites." He went on to state that "Ros is Russia, Mesheck is Muscovy, and Tubal is Tobolski. To no other country or nation can these names apply, save to that which in modern times is known by the name of "all the Russians." Nor is there any other kingdom or country that occupies a position such as would enable it to fulfill the various conditions of this prophecy, or to accomplish the work here assigned to it respecting Israel."[12] From this scant evidence, which was based solely on the similarity in sound of *rosh*, Meshech, and Tubal with Russia Moscow and Tubal, he was able to conclude that Russia was indeed the northern power spoken of by Ezekiel that would fulfill its end-times role and invade Israel. "We think therefore, that we have clearly shown that Russia is a special subject of prophecy, that is, of the prophecies of Ezekiel."[13]

Evidence of this can also be seen in John Cumming's work *The End*, also released in 1855, where he quotes from the historians of antiquity, Pliny, Josephus, and Herodotus to bolster his claims of Russia fulfilling the role of Gog in Ezekiel in 38-39. As you will read, Cumming follows a similar line of thinking as Wilhelm Gesenius in identifying rosh, Meshech, and Tubal with Russia, Moscow and Tobolsk. Cumming's claims, like those of Gesenius, are in part based on the similarity in sound of *rosh*, Meshech and Tubal with Russia, Moscow and Tobolsk:

"Pliny, the Roman writer, says, "Hierapolis, taken by the Scythians, was afterwards called Magog," one of the names given here. Josephus, the Jewish historian, says, "The

Scythians were called by the Greeks Magog."And the very name Caucasus, that we have read of so often in the papers in their accounts of recent events, is derived from the two Oriental words Gog and chasan; which means "Gog's fortified place." So that, whenever you read of the Caucasus, you read "the mountains of Gog's fortified place, or Gog's fort; "the very name of these mountains indicating the family or race with which by proximity they were intimately associated.

Meshech, another of the Scripture names, is found under the name of Moschi or the Maesi, inhabiting the Moshic mountains, east of the Black Sea. Josephus says, that the Moscheni were founded by Meshech, and the Thobelites by Tubal… Now, these two races, the descendants of Meshech and the descendants of Magog, are all found at this moment in the southern parts of the Russian Empire, in the provinces of Georgia, the Caucasus, and the Sea of Azoff, and on the Don and on the Dnieper. Their descendants penetrated into the deserts of Scythia, and peopled, subsequent to their first introduction, the northern parts of Russia. The Sarmatians, or the Muscovites, according to Herodotus, came from Pontus in Asia Minor, the very province in which they first settled, and to which we traced the descendants of Meshech and Tubal."[14]

Cumming went on to claim that the Araxes "was called in Arabic Rosh, and the people dwelling upon its banks were called by Orientals Rosh."[15] As Dwight Wilson pointed out Cumming's "argument is particularly significant because it is evidently the sources for a multitude of later writers on the subject."[16]

With the *rosh*/Russia template now in place the "*rosh*=Russia designation was introduced to a broad spectrum of Christians interested in Bible prophecy in the first edition of the *Scofield Reference Bible* in 1909 and in the revised 1917 edition."[17] Hal Lindsey popularized this template with the release of his book *The Late Great Planet Earth*. With the release of the *Left Behind* series, that now includes a newly released video game, it has been firmly entrenched in the conscience of prophetic thought. All one has to do is go back and read the works of LaHaye, Lindsey, Ice, and Hitchcock to notice how these authors use and quote the same sources. This is exactly what Hal Lindsey does in his book *The Late Great Planet Earth* where he uses the same line of reasoning as Cumming's did in *The End*. Lindsey, like Cumming, uses the same quotes from Pliny, Herodotus, and Josephus in order to make the case for the *rosh*/Russia connection. He continued to build on the *rosh*/Russia by appealing to Gesenius: "Wilhelm Gesenius, a great Hebrew scholar of the early nineteenth century, discusses these words in his unsurpassed Hebrew Lexicon. "Meshech" he says, "was founder of the Moschi, a barbarous, people who dwelt in the Moschian mountains. This scholar went on to say that the Greek name, "Moschi," derived from the Hebrew name Meshech is the source of the name for the city of Moscow." In discussing Tubal he said, "Tubal is the son of Rapheth, founder of the Tibereni a people dwelling on the Black Sea to the west of the Moschi." He finishes by saying "Gesenius concludes by saying that these people undoubtedly make up the modern Russian people."[18]

Nowhere in his books does Lindsey, along with those that have followed him, deal with how the Bible uses the word *rosh* or its relation to the ancient nations of Meshech and Tubal in the Bible.

Rosh ≠ Russia

The problem with the word *rosh* stems from how it should be understood either as a noun or as an adjective. The King James Version, Revised Standard Vision, New American Bible, and the New International Version all translate the word *rosh* as an adjective while the Jerusalem Bible, New English Bible, the LXX (Septuagint) and the New American Standard Bible translate the word *rosh* as noun and proper name. This is what modern prophecy writers do in arguing for the Russian identification in Ezekiel 38 and 39. They argue that the word *rosh* should be translated as a noun and begin looking for a name place that sounds similar to the Hebrew word *rosh*. Therefore, because the word *rosh* sounds similar to the word Russia and the aforementioned translations translate the word *rosh* as a noun and not as an adjective, it must mean that *rosh* is a specific geographical location.

Therefore, in order to further bolster the *rosh*/Russia connection, many of today's prophecy writers go to great lengths to prove the *rosh*/Russia connection. They argue that Rosh and its transliterated equivalents was a very familiar and well-known place in the ancient world supposedly living in an area to the north of the Black Sea. Supposedly the people and land of "Rosh (Rash) is identified as a place that existed as early as 2600 BC in Egyptian inscriptions. There is a later Egyptian inscription from about 1500 B.C that refers to a land called *Reshu* that was located to the north of Egypt."[19] Modern prophecy writers also like to point out that the "place name Rosh (or its phonetic equivalents in the respective languages) was found three times in the LXX, ten times in Sargon's inscriptions, once on Assurbanipal's cylinder, once in Sennacherib's annals, and five times on Ugaritic tablets— a total of twenty references in five different sources. These references to Rosh (Rashu / Reshu) demonstrate that it was a well-known land in antiquity on the banks of the Tigris River, bordering on Elam and Ellipi."[20]

Another argument put forth in support of *rosh* being viewed as a place name is based on similar sounding words found in other Semitic languages. This is known as the Canaanite shift where the word *rosh* "is pronounced *ros* in Hebrew and the Canaanite dialects, but in the other Semitic languages it is pronounced as *rasu* (Arabic), *res* (Aramaic), *ris/resu* (Ugaritic), and *resu/rosu* (Akkadian)."[21] So based on this line of argument the Hebrew word *rosh* "then becomes rashu, reshu, and rashi then finally Russia."[22]

In Genesis chapter ten, considered the Table of Nations, we find all of the players that are named in the Gog/Magog invasion of Ezekiel 38 and 39 in this chapter. Gomer, Magog, Tubal, and Meshech were the sons of Japheth. Togarmah was the son of Gomer and Javan had a son whom he named Tarshish. Ham, the second of Noah's three sons, had four sons two of which he named Put and Cush. These grandsons and great-grandsons of Noah would eventually "spread out into their territories by their clans within their nations, each with its own language" (Genesis 10:4). The one nation that is not mentioned in the table of nations is the nation of *Rosh*. The only place in the Bible where the word *rosh* is used as a proper name is in Genesis 46:21 where it is the name of Benjamin's seventh son yet no scholar has identified him with the nation of Russia.[23]

Even those that see the events of Ezekiel 38 and 39 as yet future have had to concede that "The exact name of Rosh does not appear in documents or inscriptions in ancient history. This has led many Bible scholars to believe that it is impossible to identify Rosh with any certainty... Therefore, the word *Rosh* used by Ezekiel around 585 B.C. does not refer precisely or exactly to Russia because all of the names in Ezekiel 38:2-6 refer to places that existed in Ezekiel's day."[24]

According to Dr. Edwin M. Yamauchi, "Russia comes from the word *Rus*, a Scandinavian word that was introduced into the Ukraine in the Middle Ages."[25] Dr. Yamauchi, who is a professor of history at Miami University in Oxford, Ohio, dealt extensively with the *rosh*/Russia connection in his book *Foes From the Northern Frontier*. Taking umbrage at the *rosh*/Russia connection he wrote, "it [*rosh*] can have nothing to do with modern "Russia." This would be a gross anachronism, for the modern name is based upon the name *Rus*, which was brought into the region of Kiev, north of the Black Sea, by the Vikings only in the Middle Ages."[26] He continues on, writing, "The name *Rus* or *Rhos* first occurs in the writings of the Bishop of Troyes in 839. According to the *Primary Chronicle* (compiled in the years 1037-1116), it was in the year 852 that "the land Rus (around Kiev) was first named." The "Russes" are associated with the Scandinavian Varangians in both the contemporary Russian and Arabic sources."[27]

Dr. Yamauchi is not alone in his opinion of the *rosh*/Russia connection. There are those that agree with him like Daniel Block who has stated, "The popular identification of Rosh with Russia is impossibly anachronistic and based on a faulty etymology, the assonantal similarities between Russia and Rosh being purely accidental."[28] Joseph Blenkinsopp is even more succinct in his analysis of the word *rosh* and its connection to Russia. Echoing the sentiments of the Yamauchi and Block, Blenkinsopp writes, "*ro'sh meshech* (38:2) has nothing to do, etymologically or otherwise, with Russia and Moscow...since *ro'sh* ("chief, head") is nowhere attested as such. It has no more connection with Russia (a name of Norse extraction) than Meshech has with Moscow. There is an evil empire here, but it is not [Russia]."[29] As Gary DeMar has noted "If *rosh* is a prophetic name for Russia because it sounds like Russia then why don't the other nations sound like their modern counterparts?"[30] Therefore, as Brandon Fredenburg states, the translation "the prince of Rosh" should be rejected summarily. Its inclusion is an unfortunate nod to misinformed views that identify "Rosh" as a prophetic harbinger of modern Russia. The Hebrew Masoretic text is clear: the Hebrew word *rosh* should be translated "chief" who is renamed a "prince." This yields, "Gog, of the land of Magog, the chief, the prince of Meshech and Tubal."[31]

"The fact is, since all the nations listed in Ezekiel 38 and 39 are found elsewhere in the Bible, and a nation named Rosh is not, this seems to be strong evidence that *rosh* is not being used to identify a nation or people group within the biblical context"[32] wrote Gary DeMar. "There is no need to speculate beyond the historical boundaries of Ezekiel's day to force the names of these ancient names to find a place on a modern-day map to conform them to today's geo-political landscape."[33]

Finally, Iain Duguid adds an interesting note on how to view Ezekiel 38:2:

"This phrase has been frequently translated as "prince of Rosh", where Rosh is understood as a place-name, ever since the time of the Septuagint. This translation is grammatically possible, but in the absence of any biblical evidence for such a place-name, it is better to see it as a hierarchical title, as in the similar examples of Num. 3:32 and 1 Chron. 7:40…In addition, if $r\bar{o}$'$\hat{s}$ is a part of the title, then Gog rules over a seven-nation coalition, which underlines the symbolic completeness of the forces arrayed against Israel (cf. the kinds of weapons that are subsequently burned of seven years, while the burial of Gog's army takes seen months). If $r\bar{o}$'$\hat{s}$ is a place-name, however, that symbolism is lost."[34]

The implication then is quite clear regarding the word *rosh*. If the Hebrew word *rosh* is not in any way connected with the nation of Russia, then there, is another and better way to understand how the Bible uses the word *rosh* and it connection to Ezekiel 38 and 39.

Understanding Rosh In Light of the Bible

The word *rosh* is a common Hebrew word that appears many times throughout the Old Testament that *rosh* simply means the 'head', 'chief' or 'first.'[35] Thomas Ice and Mark Hitchcock stipulate this in *The Truth Behind Left Behind* stating, "The word *Rosh* in Hebrew simply means head, top, summit, or chief. It is a very common word and is used in all Semitic languages, occurring approximately 750 times in the Old Testament, along with its roots and derivatives."[36] John MacArthur in his Bible commentary commented that *rosh* is used more than six hundred times and is best translated as "chief" or "head." Here is what he wrote in his comments regarding the word *rosh*:

"This should be translated "chief prince of Meshech and" Tubal because: (1) Rosh (more than six hundred times) in the Hebrew OT is an adjective, "chief" often in reference to the "chief priest" (2 Kings 25:18); (2) most ancient version took it to mean "chief" or "head"; and (3) in all places other than chapters 38 and 39 where both Meshech and Tubal are mentioned, Rosh is not listed as a third people (27:13; 32:26; Gen 10:2; 1 Chr 1:5).[37]

Others that have written on the topic of biblical prophecy have taken a similar stance on the word *rosh* as John MacArthur has. For example, Charles Dyer who has a very similar view on end-times prophecy as LaHaye, Hagee, Lindsey, Hitchchock, and Ice, agrees with John MacArthur on how the word *rosh* is best understood. In *The Bible Knowledge Commentary* Dyer wrote, "The evidence seems to favor taking it as an adjective. "Rosh" never appears as a nation in any other biblical list of names while all the other names are well attested."[38] Ernest Hengstenberg, who also wrote a commentary on the book of Ezekiel a few years after Gesenius and Keil, took a position that was just the opposite of Keil and Gesenius on the word *rosh*. Here are his comments on this section:

"Gog is prince over Magog, moreover *chief* prince, king of the kings over Meshech and Tubal, the Moschi and Tibareni (ch. xxvii. 13, xxxii. 26), who had their own kings, but appear here as vassals of Gog. Many expositors render, instead of chief prince, prince of Rosh, Meshech, and Tubal. But the poor Russians have been here very unjustly arranged among the enemies of God's people. Rosh, as the name of a people, does not occur in all the Old Testament."[39]

Even if we are to concede the argument to those that say the word *rosh* should be translated as noun, it does not necessarily mean that it refers to a name place. Daniel Block takes up this very argument in his work *The Book of Ezekiel: chapters 25-48.* While conceding that the syntax of 38:2 and the translation of the word *rosh* are problematic, he still translates *rosh* as a noun.[40] He translates Ezekiel 38:2 in the following way: "Human, set your face toward Gog, of the land of Magog, the prince, chief of Meshech and Tubal."[41] He justifies translating *rosh* in this way arguing that *rosh* "is best understood as a common noun, appositional to and offering a closer definition of *nāśī*. Accordingly, *the prince, chief of Mesheck and Tubal,* combines Ezekiel's preferred title for kings with a hierarchical designation, the addition serving to clarify the preceding archaic term. Ezekiel's point is that Gog is just not one of many Anatolian princely figures, but the leader among princes and over several tribal/ national groups."[42] He goes on to state that the construction found Ezekiel 38:2, "is similar to 'Pharaoh King of Egypt' in [Ezekiel] 29:2-3; 30:21-22; 31:2; 32:2."[43]

Since the Bible is its own best interpreter, we should use the Bible to find out the best way to understand how the word *rosh* is used and apply it to Ezekiel 38 and 39. "*Rosh* is used in Ezekiel 39 times and is, for example, translated as "heads" (1:22), "head"(5:1), "tops" (6:13), "chief" 27:22), and "beginning" (40:1)."[44] In Ezekiel 27:22, *rosh* refers to the chief spice that came from ancient Sheba and Ra'amah to ancient Tyre not Russian spices. In 1 Chronicles 16, David, upon bringing the Ark of the Lord to Jerusalem, appointed Levites to minister before the ark of which Asaph was chief (*rosh*) among them (1 Chronicles 16:5). In 1 Chronicles 15, Zadok, Abiathar, Uriel, Asaiah, Joel, Shemaiah, Eliel and Amminadab are called the heads (*rosh*) of the Levitical families by David. The King James Version renders it "Ye are the chief (*rosh*) of the fathers of the Levites" (1 Chronicles 15:12 KJV). In Chronicles 11 verse 6, David in the midst of trying to subdue the Jebusites stated that whoever led the attack against the Jebusites would become chief (*rosh*) and captain. Here is how the New International Version and the King James Version render this verse:

"David had said, "Whoever leads the attack on the Jebusites will become commander-in-chief." Joab son of Zeruiah went up first, and so he received the command" (NIV).

"And David said, Whosoever smiteth the Jebusites first shall be chief and captain. So Joab the son of Zeruiah went first up, and was chief" (KJV).

In 2 Samuel 8:18 David's sons were chief (*rosh*) rulers in the land of Israel. In II Chronicles 26:20 and in 31:10 Azariah is called the chief (*rosh*) priest during the reigns of Uzziah and Hezekiah. In Jeremiah 52:24, Seraiah was the chief (*rosh*) priest during the siege on Jerusalem by the Babylonians and was taken captive by Nebuzaradan along with Zephaniah who was the priest next in rank. Fast forwarding to a more contemporary time Jews today celebrate *Rosh Hashanah* because it is the chief or head holy day of the year. This is a Jewish holiday not a Russian holiday. It means "head" or "beginning" of the year and signifies the beginning of the Jewish New Year. In none of the cases cited does the Hebrew word *rosh* have any connection to the nation of Russia. With these evidences, the identifying of *rosh* with Russia is an untenable position that cannot, and should not be used as such any longer.

Meshech, Tubal and the Rest of the Gang

Meshech and Tubal, like *rosh*, were often linked to the Russian cities of Moscow and Tobolsk because of their similarity in sound. Even though many modern day prophecy writers have begun to discard this idea based on poor hermeneutics[45] there are some that still hold to this view.[46]

The names of the people groups associated with this battle are the names of ancient territories and people groups that are no longer in existence today. Dr. Yamauchi in his book *Foes From the Northern Frontier* states that the identification of Meshech and Tubal is not in doubt and any connection to Moscow and Tobolsk is simply untenable. He states that, "Since the late nineteenth century, Assyrian texts have been available which locate Mushku (Meshech) and Tabal (Tubal) in cental and eastern Anatolia respectively."[47] He also states that the names of Meshech and Tubal were preserved in Greek by one of the great historians of antiquity Herodotus "as the Moschoi and Tibarenoi tribes who lived in eastern Anatolia."[48] Josephus, like Herodotus before him, places Meshech and Tubal in the same region:

> "Thobel founded the Thobelites, who are now called Iberes (Iberians); and the Mosocheni were founded by Mosoch;

now they are Cappadocians. There is also a mark of their ancient denomination still to be shown: for there is even now among them a city called Mazaca."[49]

Meshech and Tubal were cities that were in existence in not only Ezekiel's day but in the case of Meshech going back at least as far as to the days of the prophets. In Isaiah chapter sixty-six, the LORD said that He would send some of His people to places like Tubal because they had not heard of His fame or seen His glory (66:19). In Ezekiel chapter 27, Meshech and Tubal, along with Tarshish and Beth Togarmah, are described as trading partners with the ancient city of Tyre. Greece, Tubal, and Meshech are described as trading slaves and articles of bronze for Tyre's merchandise (27:13). "This shows that Meshech and Tubal were nations that existed back then, in the 6th Century BC. Therefore they cannot possibly refer to Moscow and Tobolsk which were not founded until many centuries later."[50] This has caused even Mark Hitchcock to have to admit that, "It is highly doubtful that ancient Tyre was trading with people in the area as far north as Moscow and Tobolsk."[51]

Tarshish

Tarshish, often linked by prophecy writers to Great Britain and her satellite nations the United States, Australia, Canada, and New Zealand, amongst scholars refers to the city of Tarsus in southern Asia Minor but was most likely located in what is now Spain.Tarshish was a nation like Meshech and Tubal that existed during the days of Ezekiel and is not a reference to Great Britain or to the colonial nations, she birthed.

Tarshish has a well-established place in biblical history that goes back to the reigns of Solomon and the kings of Israel. Solomon and the kings that followed were trading partners with Tarshish bringing back gold, silver, ivory, apes, and peacocks (1 Kings 10:22; 24:48;_2 Chronicles 9:21; 2 Chronicles 20:36-37; Jeremiah 10:9). Tarshish is said to have done business with Tyre because of Tyre's great wealth. Tarshish exchanged their silver, iron, tin, and lead for Tyre's merchandise and used their ships to help export Tyre's goods (27:12, 25). According to the Bible, trade and exporting to the Mediterranean coast area was very important to the economy of Tarshish (Psalm 72:10; Isaiah 2:16; 23:1, 6, 10, 14). Jonah, in rebellion against God's orders to go to Nineveh, made plans to escape to Tarshish instead (Jonah 1:3; Jonah 4:2).

There are passages in the Bible that seem to "make it clear Tarshish lay at a distance from Judaea, and that that distance was in a north-westerly direction; and the mention of such names as Lud, Javan, and the isles, carries the mind to the extreme north-west...suggests Spain as the place for Tarshish."[52] There is nothing in the Bible that suggests that Ezekiel was talking about a nation or nations that would exist thousands of years after he originally gave this prophecy. To suggest that Tarshish is a cryptic name for Great Britain and the colonial powers that would later be birthed is simply extracting from the Bible something that is not there.

"In the Old Testament, Tarshish was the farthest western region in the known world at that time. Remember that all directions when given in the Bible, unless otherwise indicated, are to be interpreted in relationship to the land of Israel, since this is where God was working with His covenant people. Some claim that Tarshish could be used in the context to represent all the western nations from the land of Israel including Britain and those who evolved from Britain such as Canada, Australia and the Unites States. The "young lions" are taken to mean those nations such as America who stemmed from Britain. Thus, it is suggested that Tarshish with her young lions is a veiled reference to the United States. But once again this seems to strain the obvious meaning of the text and make it say much more then God ever intended it to mean (eisegesis)."[53]

Gomer

Just as Meshech and Tubal were once linked to the Russian cities of Moscow and Tobolsk by prophecy writers of the mid to late nineteenth century and all throughout the twentieth century, Gomer was often identified as the nation of Germany. The Gomer/Germany connection is often credited to the Jewish Talmud where Gomer is stated to be the Germani or the Germans. Like the Meshech and Tubal links to Moscow and Tobolsk, the Gomer link to Germany had become a commonly held view by many of the prophetic commentators during this time. So much so that commentators like Arno C. Gaebelein called it an established fact. "That the descendants of the Gomer moved northward and established themselves in parts of Germany seems to be an established fact."[54] This view held sway until the fall of the Berlin Wall forcing modern day prophecy writers like

Hal Lindsey to begin to scurry and find a replacement for Germany and once again, Turkey has become the nominee.

According to the *Histories* of Herodotus (c. 440 BC), the Cimmerians had been expelled from the steppes at some point in the past by the Scythians.[55] In his work "Herodotus related that the Cimmerians were driven south over the Caucasus, probably through the central Dariel Pass, by the Scythians in a domino like effect as the Scythians themselves were pushed westward by other tribes."[56] It appears that the ancient Cimmerians were "expelled in 700 B.C. from the southern steppes of Russia into what is today Turkey."[57] The first historical record of the Cimmerians appears in Assyrian annals in the year 714 BC. These describe how a people termed the *Gimirri* helped the forces of Sargon II to defeat the kingdom of Urartu.[58] In 652, after taking Sardis, the capital of Lydia, they reached the summit of their power. Their decline soon began, and their final defeat may be dated from 637 or 626, when they were routed by Alyattes of Lydia. Thereafter, they were no longer mentioned in historical sources but probably settled in Cappadocia, as its Armenian name, Gamir, suggests.[59]

Beth Togarmah

The Hebrew word "beth" means, "house" (cf. Eze 36:32, 37; Zec 13:1).Therefore, Beth Togarmah means house of Togarmah. Most scholars equate the name with the capital of Kammanu (Kummanni), known in Hittite texts as *Tegarama*, in Akkaddian as *Til-garimmu* and in classical sources as Gauraena (modern Gurun). Togarmah was both the name of a district and a city in the border of Tubal in eastern Cappadocia. Togarmah was known variously in history as Tegarma, Tagarma, and Takarama. The ancient Assyrians referred to this city as Til-garimmu. One of the maps of the Cambridge Ancient History locates Til-garimmu on the northeast border of Tubal in the northeast part of modern Turkey.[60] Located "in the remotest part of the north" (Ezek 38:6), on the border of Tubal, this region was renowned for its horse breeding.[61] In Ezekiel chapter 27, Beth Togarmah is said to exchange work horses, war horses and mules with Tyre for its merchandise (27:14).

Persia, Put, and Cush

The ancient people of Cush "lived in the southern part of the modern day Egypt and the northern part of the present day

Sudan."[62] The term "Kush" (Cush) was used by the ancient Egyptians to designate one of the states to the south of their frontier at the First Cataract. Modern scholars have equated the Kingdom of Cush with the culture base at the town of Kerma in northern Sudan.[63] It was this people group, who lived primarily in the southern part of the modern day Egypt and northern part of the present day Sudan, that the Greek historians Herodotus and Diodorus Siculus and Roman historian Strabo called the "Aithiopians" or "Ethiopians."[64]

Put is mentioned in the Bible in Ezekiel 27:10 as serving in the army of Tyre along with Persia and Lydia and in the book of Nahum along with Cush and Libya as the defender of the Egyptian city of Thebes (Nah 3:7-9). Nahum lists Put and Libya as separate people groups and the fact that they are listed together may suggest that they are associated with one another maybe even bordering each other. Put is often identified with ancient Libya typically identified with regions that were west of the Nile Valley and generally corresponding to modern Northwest Africa. Josephus links Put with ancient Libya in his work *Antiquities of the Jews*:

"Phut also was the founder of Libya, and called the inhabitants Phutites, from himself: there is also a river in the country

of Moors which bears that name; whence it is that we may
see the greatest part of the Grecian historiographers mention
that river and the adjoining country by the apellation of Phut:
but the name it has now has been by change given it from
one of the sons of Mesraim, who was called Lybyos."[65]

Ancient Libya "was often mainly identified as the lands west
of Ancient Egypt, the home of tribes, or peoples, like the
Meshwesh, Peywed, Libu, Tamahu and Garmantians. To a
large extent Ancient Libya began in its east with Siwa Oasis
(Egypt) and ending in central modern Tunisia, but possibly
covering extensive areas into modern Algeria."[66]

Persia is well attested in history and there is no dispute
regarding the ancient nation. The first Persian Empire formed
under the Median Empire (728–559 BC) after defeating and
ending the Assyrian Empire with the help of Babylonians.
The Achaemenid Persian Empire (550–330 BC) was the
largest empire of the ancient world and it reached its greatest
extent under Darius the Great and Xerxes the Great — famous
in antiquity as the foe of the classical Greek states (See
Greco-Persian Wars). It was a united Persian kingdom that
originated in the region now known as Pars province (Fars
province) of Iran. It was formed under Cyrus the Great, who

took over the empire of the Medes, and conquered much of the Middle East, including the territories of the Babylonians, Assyrians, the Phoenicians, and the Lydians.[67] When Ezekiel wrote this prophecy in the sixth century B.C., these nations would eventually fall within the boundaries of the Persian Empire as would have Put (Libya) and Cush (Sudan). The Macmillan Bible Atlas includes Put (Libya) in the territorial boundaries of the Persian Empire[68] which had 127 provinces that stretched from India to Ethiopia (Cush).[69]

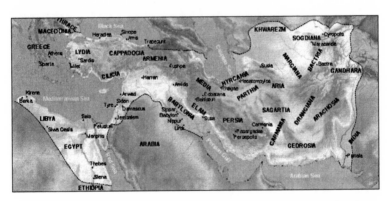

Achaemenid Empire at its greatest extent under Emperor Darius the Great in 500 B.C.

The names of these ancient people groups and civilizations are not cryptic allusions to the modern day nations of Turkey, Iran, Germany, Sudan, Libya or Russia and its cities Moscow and Tobolsk. These ancient people groups existed in Ezekiel's day and those of his readers. "The nations then located in the area that is now Turkey, Syria, northern Iran and Iraq, and western Russia were nations when Persia and Greece were in power in the second century B.C. in terms of Israel's location , these land masses constituted the "far north." An area between the Black and Caspian Seas was certainly far north in terms of Israel's location."[70] They would have been very familiar with these names and their geographical locations. "There is no need to speculate beyond the historical boundaries of Ezekiel's day to force the names of these ancient nations to find a place on the modern-day map to conform them to today's geo-political landscape."[71] As E. W. Hengstenberg once stated, "To seek the fulfillment in the dark region of the end of the days is the less possible, because most of the nations named either no longer exist, or are no longer heathen. Magog, Gomer, Meshech and Tubal, Phut, Sheba, and Dedan, are no more to be found."[72]

If Ezekiel 38 and 39 is not a prophecy about the much talked about Russian Confederacy, who then is the invader coming from the north. The short answer is Haman. A biblical case can be made that the invader being prophesied about in Ezekiel 38 and 39 is none other than the infamous and evil Haman.

Notes

[1] Arno C. Gaebelein, *The Harmony of the Prophetic Word: A Key To Old Testament Prophecy Concerning Things To Come* (New York: Fleming H. Revell Company, 1907), p.67

[2] John F. Walvoord, *Israel In Prophecy* (Grand Rapids, MI: Zondervan, 1962), p.129

[3] Gary DeMar, *Why the End of the World is Not in Your Future: Identifying the Gog-Magog Alliance* (Powder Springs, GA: American Vision Press, 2008), p.69

[4] ibid, 69

[5] Tim LaHaye and Jerry B. Jenkins, *Are We Living in the End Times?* (Carol Stream, IL: Tyndale House, 1999), p.86

[6] Gary DeMar, *Last Days Madness: Obsession of the Modern Church*, 4th ed. (Powder Springs, GA: American Vision, 1999) p.363

[7] Tim LaHaye, *The Beginning Of The End* (Wheaton, IL: Tyndale House, 1972), p.62

[8] Gary DeMar, *Why the End of the World is Not in Your Future*, p.101

[9] http://www.blueletterbible.org/study/lexica/gesenius/

[10] Wilhelm Gesenius, *A Hebrew and English Lexicon of the Old Testament, Including the Biblical Chaldee*, trns. Edward Robinson (Boston: Crocker and Brewster, 1871), p.955

[11] Wilhelm Gesenius is not the only "authority" that modern day prophecy writers appeal to. They also appeal to eighteenth

century Bible commentator Bishop William Lowth, C.F. Keil, and G. A. Cooke.

[12] John Gaylord, *The Future of Russia, or an Answer to the Question, How Will the Great Eastern Struggle Finally Terminate?*, (Milwaukee: S.M. Booth, 1855), p.20

[13] ibid, p.20

[14] John Cumming, *The End: The Proximate Signs Of The Close Of This Dispensation* (John P. Jewett and Company, 1855) p.199-200

[15] ibid, p.200-201

[16] Dwight Wilson, *Armageddon Now!: The Premillenarian Response to Russia and Israel Since 1917* (Tyler, TX: Institute for Christian Economics, [1977] 1991), p.27

[17] Gary DeMar, *Why the End of the World is Not in Your Future*, p.76

[18] Hal Lindsey, *The Late Great Planet Earth* (Grand Rapids, MI: Zondervan, 1970), p.64-66

[19] Mark Hitchcock, *Iran: The Coming Crisis* (Sisters, OR: Multnomah Press, 2006), p.162. Modern day prophecy writers insist that the Russia must be the nation spoke of by Ezekiel because it is the only nation that is 'far north' of Israel (38:6, 15; 39:2). Using the same argument against modern day prophecy teachers, if you draw a line directly due north of Egypt, the country that is in 'the remotest part of the north' from Egypt is not Russia. The nation that is the furthest north of Egypt is Finland. Yet there is not discussion of how the nation of how Finland fits into the end-times Gog/Magog scenario.

[20] James D. Price, "Rosh: An Ancient Land Known to Ezekiel," *Grace Theological Journal* (1985), p. 71-73. http://gts.grace.edu/documents/Price-Rosh-Ezekiel-GTJ.pdf. Also see Mark Hitchcock, *Iran: The Coming Crisis* (Sisters, OR: Multnomah Press, 2006), p.162. However, the statement that the name place Rosh "was a well-known land in antiquity on the banks of the Tigris River, bordering on Elam and Ellipi" does great damage to modern day prophecy writers that insist that Russia is the nation being prophesied by Ezekiel in chapters 38 & 39 based on its northern geographical location. The land of Elam was located in modern day Iran which is due east of Israel and not north. The Elamite civilization was located in the southwestern portion of what is now modern day Iran. (http://creationwiki.org/Elam).

[21] ibid, p.69-70. A similar argument is put forth by Clyde E. Billington in a three part article that appeared in the Michigan Theological Journal: "The Rosh People in History and Prophecy." Billington stated that the "Rosh people who lived to the north of the Black Sea in ancient and medieval times were called the Rus/Ros/Rox/Aorsi from very early times." Clyde E. Billington, "The Rosh People in History and Prophecy," *Michigan Theological Journal* (1993), p.61

[22] Gary DeMar, *Why the End of the World is Not in Your Future*, p.70

[23] That is yet! Modern day prophecy writers are married to the idea that Russia along with its confederates will one day invade Israel. They are so married to this idea they have gone through great lengths to prove that Russia is indeed the nation Ezekiel was talking about in his prophecy to the point of boxing themselves in with absolutely no ability to divorce themselves from this view and come up with an alternative view. Considering that modern day prophecy writers go to great lengths to prove the *rosh*=Russia connection, the

question must be asked. How soon will it be before modern prophecy writers begin to link Jews that migrated and eventually settled in Russia with Benjamin's son Rosh in order to continue to maintain and insist that Russia is the nation being prophesied in Ezekiel 38 and 39?

[24] Mark Hitchcock, *After the Empire: Bible Prophecy in Light of the Fall of the Soviet Union* (Wheaton, Ill: Tyndale House, 1994), p.31-32

[25] Edwin M. Yamauchi, "Updating the Armageddon Calendar," *Christianity Today* (April 29, 1991), p.51 Quoted in Gary DeMar, *Last Days Madness: Obsession of the Modern Church*, 4th ed. (Powder Springs, GA: American Vision, 1999), p.364

[26] Edwin Yamauchi, *Foes From the Northern Frontier: Invading Hordes from the Russian Steppes* (Eugene, OR: Wipf and Stock, [1982] 2003), p.20

[27] ibid, 21

[28] Daniel I. Block, *The Book of Ezekiel: chapters 25-48* (Grand Rapids, MI: Wm. B. Eerdmans, 1998), p.434

[29] Joseph Blenkinsopp, *Ezekiel: Interpretation, a Bible Commentary for Teaching and Preaching* (Louisville, KY: John Knox Press, 1990), p.181, 184

[30] Gary DeMar, *Last Days Madness*, p.366

[31] Brandon Fredenburg, *The College Press NIV Commentary: Ezekiel* (Joplin, MO: College Press Publishing Company, 2002), p.337

[32] Gary DeMar, *Why the End of the World is Not in Your Future*, p.71

[33] ibid, p.71

[34] Iain M. Duguid, *Ezekiel: The NIV Application Commentary* (Grand Rapids, MI: Zondervan , 1999), p.448

[35] According to Strong's Concordance: 7218 ro'sh roshe from an unused root apparently; the head (as most easily shaken), whether literal or figurative (in many applications, of place, time, rank, itc.):—band, beginning, captain, chapiter, chief(-est place, man, things), company, end, X every (man), excellent, first, forefront, ((be-))head, height, (on) high(-est part, (priest)), X lead, X poor, principal, ruler, sum, top. James Strong, *The New Strong's Exhaustive Concordance of the Bible*, (Nashville, TN; Thomas Nelson Publishers, 1996)

[36] Mark Hitchcock and Thomas Ice, *The Truth Behind Left Behind: A Biblical View of the End Times* (Sisters, OR: Multnomah Press, 2004), p.49

[37] John MacArthur, "Ezekiel," *The MacArthur Bible Commentary* (Nashville, TN: Thomas Nelson, 2005), p. 933

[38] Charles Dyer, "Ezekiel," *The Bible Knowledge Commentary: Old Testament*, eds. John Walvoord and Roy Zuck (David C Cook, 1985), p.1299. ©1985 Cook Communications Ministries. *Bible Knowledge Commentary: Old Testament* by Walvoord and Zuck. Used with permission. May not be further reproduced. All rights reserved.

[39] Ernst Wilhelm Hengstenberg, *The Prophecies of the Prophet Ezekiel Elucidated* (Edinburgh: T &T Clark, 1869), p.333

[40] Daniel I. Block, The Book of Ezekiel: Chapters 25-48, p.434

[41] ibid, p.432

[42] ibid, p.435

[43] ibid, p.435

[44] Gary DeMar, *Why the End of the World is Not in Your Future*, p.78

[45] Mark Hitchcock, *After the Empire*, p.56-58

[46] John Hagee, *Jerusalem Countdown: A Warning to the World,* (Lake Mary, FL: Frontline, 2006), p.104

[47] Edwin Yamauchi, *Foes From the Northern Frontier*, p.25

[48] ibid, 23

[49] Flavius Josephus, *The Antiquities of the Jews* 1.6.1. *Josephus: The Complete Works*, trns. William Whiston (Nashville, TN: Thomas Nelson, 1998)

[50] Thomas Williamson, "Will There Be a Russian Invasion of Israel?": http://thomaswilliamson.net/russian_invasion.htm

[51] Mark Hitchcock, *The Coming Islamic Invasion of Israel* (Sisters, OR: Multnomah Press, 2002), p.45

[52] *A Cyclopædia of Biblical Literature*, "Tarshish" eds. John Kitto and William Lindsay Alexander 3 vol. (Edinburgh: Adam and Charles Black, 1876), 3:966. The Bible says that it took three years for the ships of Solomon to return from Tarshish with their cargo (1 Kings 10:22).

[53] Kelly Sensenig, "America in Bible Prophecy": http://tinyurl.com/3s5bm4

[54] Arno C. Gabelein, *The Annotated Bible: The Holy Scriptures Analyzed and Annotated* (New York: Our Hope, 1921), p.320

[55] http://www.statemaster.com/encyclopedia/Cimmerians

[56] Edwin Yamauchi, *Foes From the Northern Frontier*, p.50

[57] Jennifer Rast, "The Coming War of Gog and Magog, an Islamic Invasion?": http://www.contenderministries.org/prophecy/gogmagog.php

[58] http://www.statemaster.com/encyclopedia/Cimmerians

[59] "Cimmerian." Encyclopædia Britannica. 2009. Encyclopædia Britannica Online. 20 Jul. 2009 <http://www.britannica.com/EBchecked/topic/117922/Cimmerian>. Josephus claims that Gomer should be identified with the Celtic Galatians (Antiquities1.6.1) although Dr. Yamauchi states that this identification is anachronistic. Edwin Yamauchi, *Foes From the Northern Frontier: Invading Hordes from the Russian Steppes*, p.49. The Galatians were in their origin a part of that great Celtic migration which invaded Macedonia, led by the 'second' Brennus, a Gaulish chief. He invaded Greece in 281 BCE with a huge warband and was turned back in the nick of time from plundering the temple of Apollo at Delphi. At the same time, another Gaulish group were migrating with their women and children through Thrace. They had split off from Brennus' Gauls in 279 BCE, and had migrated into Thrace under their leaders Leonnorius and Lutarius. These Gaulish invaders appeared in Asia Minor in 278– 277 BCE. As so often happens in cases of invasion, the invaders came at the express invitation of Nicomedes I of Bithynia, who required help in a dynastic struggle against his brother. Three tribes of Gauls crossed over from Thrace to Asia Minor. They numbered about 10,000 fighting men and about the same number of women and children, divided into three tribes, Trocmi, Tolistobogii and Tectosages.

The migration led to the establishment of a long-lived Gaulish territory in central Anatolia, which included the eastern part of ancient Phrygia, a territory that became known as Galatia. There they ultimately settled, and being strengthened by fresh accessions of the same clan from Europe, they overran Bithynia, and supported themselves by plundering neighboring countries. http://www.masterliness.com/a/Galatia.htm

[60] Mark Hitchcock, *After the Empire*, p.63-64

[61] Daniel I. Block, *The Book of Ezekiel: chapters 25-48*, p.73-74

[62] Dr. Wolassa L. Kumo, "Kush, Nubia, Ethiopia and Sudan: Ancient Civilisations and Modern Nomenclature: Part I," *American Chronicle* (April 13, 2009): http://www.american-chronicle.com/articles/view/98270

[63] *Encyclopedia of African History*, "Kush," ed. Kevin Shillington vol. 1 (New York: Fitzroy Dearborn Taylor & Francis Group, 2004), p.781

[64] Dr. Wolassa L. Kumo, "Kush, Nubia, Ethiopia and Sudan"

[65] Flavius Josephus, *The Antiquities of the Jews* 1.6.2

[66] http://looklex.com/e.o/libya_a.htm

[67] http://en.wikipedia.org/wiki/Persian_Empire

[68] Gary DeMar, "The Fiction Behind Left Behind", *Worldview Magazine* (July 2004), p.16

[69] Flavius Josephus, *The Antiquities of the Jews*, 11.6.6.

[70] Gary DeMar, *Last Days Madness*, p.365

[71] Gary DeMar, *Why the End of the World is Not in Your Future*, p.71

[72] Ernst Wilhelm Hengstenberg, *The Prophecies of the Prophet Ezekiel Elucidated*, p.331

CHAPTER SEVEN

Ezekiel 37 and the Reconstitution of Israel: Fulfilled or Unfulfilled

—ᗩᗯ—

In March 2005, Israel's Chief Rabbi Shlomo Amar formally announced that Israel was officially going to recognize the Bnei Menashe as part of the lost tribe of Manasseh, one of the Ten Lost Tribes of Israel, and could therefore begin to immigrate to Israel under the Law of Return. This was big news for assiduous prophecy students as it was seen as fulfilling Ezekiel's proclamation: "This is what the Sovereign LORD says: I will take the Israelites out of the nations where they have gone. I will gather them from all around and bring them back into their own land. I will make them one nation in the land, on the mountains of Israel. There will be one king over all of them and they will never again be two nations or be divided into two kingdoms" (Ezekiel 37:21-22). This same excitement at the return of the lost tribe of Manasseh was exhibited in the early 1990's when Ethiopian Jews began immigrating back to the nation of Israel. This return to Israel was seen as prophetic fulfillment of God's promise to return the Jews from all the nations where they had been exiled.

All the Nations

The return of the Jews to Israel from all over the world has been hailed by many Christians as prophetic fulfillment of God's promise to return the Jews from all the nations where they had been exiled. They point to the return of the Bnei Menashe and Ethiopian Jews as a sign that the prophesied return of the Jews including the Ten Lost Tribes of Israel to their homeland is being fulfilled right before our eyes. There are Christian ministries that have been setup with the sole purpose of helping repatriate Jews back to Israel from all over world. God, through the prophet Ezekiel, said that Gog and his confederates would come against the land of

Israel "whose people had been gathered from many nations" (Ezekiel 38:8). Ezekiel was prophesying about a time in the future when God would restore the Jews to their homeland "from many nations."[1] It is naturally assumed that since the Jews are returning from nations all over the world, ""all the nations" must refer to every nation in the world"[2] found on a modern map. However, the Bible's use of the phrases "all the nations" and "every nation" is quite different from our modern understanding of how the Bible uses these phrases.

The phrases "all the nations," "to the nations," "among the nations," and "every nation" does not necessarily mean every nation in the world found on a modern map but "are descriptions of the known world that was ruled by kingdoms that incorporated nations into their political orbit."[3] For example, God forewarned the Israelites that if they were not obedient to his covenant that they would be exiled "among the nations" (Leviticus 26:33, 38; Deuteronomy 4:27, 30:1; Nehemiah 1:8; Jeremiah 30:11; Ezekiel 11:16-17; 12:15; 36:19-23). When Jeremiah was tasked by God to take the cup of His wrath to "all the nations" (Jer. 25:15), it would be a far stretch to think that this means our world today. The succeeding verses tell us exactly which nations were to receive the cup of God's wrath. They were Jerusalem and the towns of Judah (v18), Pharaoh king of Egypt and all his people (v19), all the kings of Uz; all the kings of the Philistines (v20), Edom, Moab and Ammon (v21), all the kings of Tyre and Sidon, (v22) along with all of the kings from the coastland to the desert stretching from Dedan to Media (v23-26). These are nations and people groups that existed in the days of Jeremiah and Ezekiel and aren't code words for modern day nation states.

Remember that in 586 B.C. King Nebuchadnezzar destroyed the kingdom of Judah, the temple, and the city of Jerusalem. Just as Ezekiel was prophesying to the first set of Jewish exiles in Babylon, Jeremiah was at the same time prophesying to the Jews in Jerusalem. "The dates of his ministry, which spanned five decades, are from the Judean king Josiah's thirteenth year, noted in 1:2 (627 B.C.), to beyond the fall of Jerusalem to Babylon in 586 B.C. (Jer. 39; 40; 52)."[4] Keep in mind that the book of Jeremiah and the book of Lamentations were written during the siege of Jerusalem by Nebuchadnezzar. Jeremiah in the book of Lamentations states, "Judah has gone into exile. She dwells among the nations...Her king and her princes are exiled among the nations" (Lamentations 1:3; Lamentations 2:9, cf. Ezekiel 12:16). Jeremiah, in a letter sent to the exiles in Babylon, in chapter twenty-nine states where the Lord says, "I will be found by you," declares the LORD, "and will bring you back from captivity. [b] I will gather you from all the nations and places where I have banished you" (Jeremiah 29:14). These nations were nations that encompassed Israel and were eventually incorporated by the geo-political powers of their day. Therefore, the places where the Jews had been banished was Assyria and the nations that made up the Assyrian Empire (2 Kings 17:6) and Babylon and the nations that made up the Babylonian Empire which including Assyria and ultimately became the Medo-Persian Empire (see Esther 3:8; 8:11-13; 9:1-5, 11-12, 16, 19).

A perfect example of this can be found in the books of Daniel and Ezra. Both Nebuchadnezzar, king of Babylon, and Cyrus, king of Persia, are said to be rulers over all of the nations and kingdoms of the earth. Nebuchadnezzar, in a communiqué sent throughout the Babylonian empire sends it "To the peoples, nations and men of every language, who live in all the world" (Daniel 4:1). Cyrus in giving the proclamation for the Jews to return home to Jerusalem and Judah and begin rebuilding the temple stated, "The LORD, the God of heaven, has given me all the kingdoms of the earth and he has appointed me to build a temple for him at Jerusalem in Judah" (Ezra 1:2).

In Jeremiah 34:1, where Nebuchadnezzar's army is said to be made up of "all the kingdoms and peoples in the empire he ruled," says that the nations that made up the Babylonian army "were fighting against Jerusalem and all its surrounding towns." So when we read in Zechariah chapters 12 and 14 how all the nations will be gathered against Jerusalem to fight against it, there is no need to infer from scripture that "all the nations" is a reference to every single modern day nation coming against Israel during the Tribulation as modern prophecy writers assert.

Based on the context of Daniel 4:1, Ezra 1:2, and 34:1, it's safe to say that the reference to all the nations coming against Israel describes the armies of nations and kingdoms that had been conquered and grafted into the geo-political power of Zechariah's day; more than likely the Persians.

The regathering of Israel: In belief or Unbelief?

There is a raging debate within certain circles of Christianity on whether or not the re-establishment of modern day Israel is fulfilling biblical prophecy. Modern prophecy writers point to the return of the Jews back to Israel, including elements of the Ten Lost Tribes of Israel as proof that (1) we are in the last days and (2) that God is keeping His promises to the Jews by returning them to the Promised Land. The return of the Jews to Israel according, to modern prophecy teachers, fulfills biblical verses that deal with the return of the Jews such as, Ezekiel. 20:33-38; 22:17-22; 36:22-24; 37:1-14; Isaiah.11:11-12. However, the heart of the issue surrounds the spiritual state of the Jews upon returning to the land of Israel; whether the return of the Jews to Israel was to happen in unbelief or belief.

Earlier writers on prophecy, like Thomas M. Chalmers, believed that any return to the Promised Land by the Jews was predicated on the prerequisite necessity of their conversion to Christianity.[5] Christian periodicals like *The Sunday School Time* took a different view arguing that the Scriptures conclusively show that the Jews would return to the Promised Land in unbelief.[6] Today, modern prophecy writers argue from both ends of the spectrum. In order for modern day Israel to be prophetically significant and yet fulfill the biblical mandate of repentance before restoration, modern day prophecy writers argue for two gatherings: one in unbelief and the other in belief. This was the argument taken up by Mark Hitchcock and Thomas Ice in *The Truth Behind Left Behind*.[7] They argue that the "first worldwide regathering will be a return in unbelief, in preparation for the judgment of the Tribulation. The second worldwide regathering will be a return in faith at the end of the Tribulation, in preparation for the blessing of the Millennium, or the thousand year reign of Christ"[8] but only after two-thirds of the Jews perish in the land of Israel[9] at the hands of Antichrist's forces. The question is how the Bible deals with the issue of Jewish restoration to the land of Israel.

The books of Leviticus and Deuteronomy clearly spells out the stipulations of any God ordained Jewish return to the land of Israel. Any return to the land must be done so in accordance with the conditions described in Leviticus 26:40-42, Deuteronomy 4:27-31, and 30:1-8:

"But if they will confess their sins and the sins of their fathers — their treachery against me and their hostility toward me,[41] which made me hostile toward them so that I sent them into the land of their enemies — then when their uncircumcised hearts are humbled and they pay for their sin,[42] I will remember my covenant with Jacob and my covenant with

Isaac and my covenant with Abraham, and **I will remember the land**." (Leviticus 26:40-42)

"The LORD will scatter you among the peoples, and only a few of you will survive among the nations to which the LORD will drive you.[28] There you will worship man-made gods of wood and stone, which cannot see or hear or eat or smell.[29] **But if from there you seek the LORD your God, you will find him if you look for him with all your heart and with all your soul**.[30] When you are in distress and all these things have happened to you, **then in later days you will return to the LORD your God and obey him.**[31] For the LORD your God is a merciful God; he will not abandon or destroy you or forget the covenant with your forefathers, which he confirmed to them by oath." (Deuteronomy 4:27-31)

"When all these blessings and curses I have set before you come upon you and you take them to heart wherever the LORD your God disperses you among the nations,[2] and **when you and your children return to the LORD your God and obey him with all your heart and with all your soul according to everything I command you today,[3] then**

**the LORD your God will restore your fortunes and have
compassion on you and gather you again from all the
nations where he scattered you.**[4] **Even if you have been
banished to the most distant land under the heavens, from
there the LORD your God will gather you and bring you
back.**[5] **He will bring you to the land that belonged to your
fathers, and you will take possession of it**. He will make
you more prosperous and numerous than your fathers.[6] The
LORD your God will circumcise your hearts and the hearts
of your descendants, so that you may love him with all your
heart and with all your soul, and live.[7] The LORD your
God will put all these curses on your enemies who hate and
persecute you.[8] **You will again obey the LORD and follow
all his commands I am giving you today."** (Deuteronomy
30:1-8)

When the book of Deuteronomy is read in a literal fashion,
it is very clear that repentance *is always* the condition of
return. In his comments on the book of Deuteronomy, J.A.
Thompson makes this very point:

"If in exile the people turned to Yahweh again, He would
have compassion on them and they would be restored to

enjoy yet greater blessings...in exile Israel would take to heart the covenant sanctions, the blessings and the curses, and would return to Yahweh to obey His voice with all their heart, i.e. completely...Israel will be restored to her land when she turns to Yahweh with all her heart, for He will *restore your fortunes, and have compassion upon you...*The reference is to a radical change in Israel's conditions...In his *compassion (rahᵃmim)* Yahweh will gather His people from the lands to which they have been driven. The total picture is of a repentant people being restored to their homeland, a very different picture from that which obtains in modern Israel, where there is little evidence of repentance and where great numbers of people are agnostic."[10]

Peter C. Craigie outlines the process from repentance to restoration in the following way:

(a) *You shall return to your senses* (v.1)—the people would remember that the circumstances in which they found themselves were not the result of "fate," but an inevitable consequence of disobeying the covenant with the Lord, which resulted in the curse of the Lord.

(b) *Return to the Lord* (v.2)—once they knew the reason for the curse that had befallen them, the course of action would become clear. In repentance, they must return to the Lord of the Covenant, individually and as families.

(c) *You shall listen to his voice* (v.2)—the repentance involved not only turning back from evil past, but a new and wholehearted commitment of obedience to God's voice, which was expressed for them in God's and was written in a book (see v.10).

(d) *Then the Lord your God will restore you fortunes* (v.3)— the nature of exile would be such that repentance alone could not lead to freedom, for the people would be in foreign lands under foreign authorities. Having remembered, repented, and obeyed, then the people could look to God for his aid in restoring them to that previous position...[11]

Evidence of the repentance needed to return to the land of Israel is found in the Bible in the books of Daniel and Nehemiah (Daniel 9:1-19; Nehemiah 1:4-11; 9:1-38). Both Daniel and Nehemiah are examples of the repentance required, both corporately and individually, in order for Jewish restoration to the land to be a reality. Therefore, on the basis of Deuteronomy 30 and from a New Testament perspective, the required recognition of Jesus as Messiah is the condition to any "right" of return. In order for Jewish return to the land of Israel to be prophetically significant there has to be repentance. The Jews must return to the Lord and His Covenant, individually and as families"[12] (see Ezra 10:1; Daniel 9:20).

The Ten Lost Tribes of Israel According to the Bible

Ezekiel 37 is a prophecy about the resurrection and restoration of the nation of Israel. Verses 21 and 22 goes on to state that the once divided nation of Israel (Southern Kingdom and Northern Kingdom) would return from exile united as one nation. However, we see the fulfillment of these events in the book of Ezra. Ezra states that the exiles returned united as one nation: "'Now when the seventh month came, and the sons of Israel were in the cities, the people gathered together as one man to Jerusalem" (Ezra 3:1, NASB). We are told Ezra in 6:16-17 and again in 8:35 how the exiles offered "twelve bulls for all Israel" (8:35) and "twelve male goats, one for each of the tribes of Israel" (6:16-17) as a sin offering for all Israel. In the New Testament, we see references to tribes that were supposedly lost to history. Matthew 4:13-16 mentions the tribes of Nephtali and Zebulun, Luke mentions that the prophetess Anna was from the tribe of Asher (Luke 2:36), and Paul in his testimony before Herod Agrippa mentioned how the twelve tribes of Israel "earnestly serve God day and night" in hope of seeing the promise to the patriarchs fulfilled (Acts 26:7).

The evidence from the Bible indicates that none of the twelve tribes have been lost to history. It seems that many from the ten northern tribes lived amongst the southern tribes before the Babylonian exile (see. 2 Chron. 11:3; 31:6) and returned to the land of Israel along with their southern brethren after the time of the exile had passed.

Out of the North He Comes

John Hagee in his book *Beginning of the End*, Hagee equates the Jews that are returning to Israel from the "north country" with Russia.[13] The argument for Russia being the prophesied "north country" is as follows: Since Russia is the only country on a map that is to the extreme north of Israel (38:6, 15; 39:2) then it must mean that this is the nation prophesied by the prophet Ezekiel in chapters 38 and 39. While it is true that Russia does lie to the far north of Israel, "it is incorrect to infer that because Russia is the nation farthest north of Israel, it is the one meant in the Bible."[14]

The Bible's use of 'north' has different designations and none of them has any reference to the nation of Russia. For example, the Bible states that God and His dwelling place are said to reside in the north. According to Job, "**Out of the north** he comes in golden splendor; God comes in awesome majesty" (Job 37:22). In Ezekiel chapter one, Ezekiel in a vision saw the Lord coming from the north. Of this vision he says, "I looked, and I saw a windstorm coming **out of the north**—an immense cloud with flashing lightning and surrounded by brilliant light" (Ezekiel 1:4). Mount Zion God's holy hill is said to lay in the far north: "Beautiful in elevation, the joy of the whole earth, is Mount Zion **in the far north**, the city of the great King" (Psalms 48:2, NASB).

Not only does the Bible use north as a designation for God's dwelling place but it also uses north as a designation for geographical areas that are to the east and northeast of Israel. For example, Jeremiah 46:20-26 is a warning to Egypt and its Pharaoh Neco II regarding the punishment that was coming from the north. Jeremiah clearly states that this punishment will be at the hand of King Nebuchadnezzar: "Egypt is a beautiful heifer, but a gadfly is coming against her **from the north**... I will hand them over to those who seek their lives, to Nebuchadnezzar king of Babylon and his officers" (Jeremiah 46:20, 26). This same northern designation is used by Ezekiel to describe Tyre's overthrow by the Babylonians (26:7) and by Jeremiah and Isaiah to describe the Persian Empire's conquest and overthrow of the Babylonian Empire (Isaiah 41:25; Jeremiah 50:1-3; 8-10; 41-46; 51:1-12, 27-28, 48). God used Babylon and Persia along with Assyria as agents of vengeance (Isaiah 10:4; 41:25; Jeremiah 1:13-16; 3:18; 6:1, 22; 50:41-46; 51:1-12). David Chilton made a statement regarding this that is very insightful: "It should be remembered too that the *north* was the area of God's throne (Isaiah 14:13); and both the Glory-Cloud and God's agents of vengeance are seen coming from the north, i.e., from the Euphrates (cf. Ezekiel 1:4; Isaiah 14:31; Jeremiah 1:14-15). Thus, this great army from the north is ultimately *God's* army, and under His control and direction, although it is also plainly demonic and pagan in character..."[15]

In Jeremiah 4:6, God said that He was bringing destruction from the north against the kingdom of Judah. This passage is a prophecy regarding the Babylonian Empire under King Nebuchadnezzar and his destruction of the kingdom of Judah in 586 B.C. Jeremiah 25:9 is very clear that Nebuchadnezzar is coming from the north against Judah:

> **"I will summon all the peoples of the north and my servant Nebuchadnezzar king of Babylon,"** declares the LORD, "and I will bring them against this land and its inhabitants and against all the surrounding nations. I will completely destroy them and make them an object of horror and scorn, and an everlasting ruin."

Many other passages in Jeremiah predict the coming of the Babylonians from the north to besiege Judah and Jerusalem prior to their destruction in 586 B.C. yet the capitol city of the Babylonian empire, Babylon, was to the east of Israel (Jeremiah 1:13-16; 3:18; 6:1, 22; 10:22; 23:7; 25:9; cf. Zechariah 2:6-7). Even Charles Dyer agrees that the "foe from the north" is an "apt description of the Babylonians (cf. Hab. 1:6-11),"[16] even though he believes that the events described in Ezekiel 38 and 39 are yet future. He goes on to say that "the disaster from the north that was bringing destruction" was the "approaching army of Babylon in its ferocity was like a lion that had come out of his lair to attack the land of Judah."[17] The implication is quite clear, since Babylon is prophesied invading Israel from the north while being east of Israel, then Ezekiel's use of the same northern designation in chapters 38 and 39 can in turn have the same meaning. As Timothy Dailey pointed out, "From the perspective of the Holy Land, the invaders came down from the north, even if their place of origin was actually to the east. Ezekiel is giving the *direction* of the invasion, not the invader's place of origin."[18]

The editors of the *NIV Study Bible* support this statement by Dailey. In the notes on Isaiah 41:25 it says, "From the perspective of those living in Jerusalem, invasions came primarily from the north."[19] This was the case when the Assyrian Empire under Shalmaneser came from the north and laid siege and exiled the northern kingdom of Israel in 722 B.C. (II Kings17:3-6). When Nero gave the imperial edict to Vespasian to officially go to war with the Jews in February/ March A.D.67, Vespasian started his military campaign from the north in the Galilee region. One of the first cities to fall in the beginning stages of Vespasian's campaign to put down the Jewish revolt was the city of Jotapata that was located just north of Cana and to the south and west of Capernaum. ""North" refers not so much to the precise geographical direction from Israel, but rather to the direction of advance and attack upon Israel (armies came against Israel from the north). This is how Jeremiah viewed Babylonia, though Babylonia was technically to the east. Consequently there is no firm basis on which to interpret Gog as Russia."[20]

Fred Zaspel has a noteworthy observation regarding the northern designation found in Ezekiel 38:6: "One more fact is worthy of observation here. In verse 6 [of Ezekiel 38] this same geographical description ("farthest north") is also given of Togarmah, yet virtually all agree that this is eastern Asia Minor! If Asia Minor was far north enough for Togarmah, why not for Gog? The problem is obvious." He goes on to say, "Moreover, if Asia Minor is not the "farthest north," then why stop with Russia? Why not go on to the north pole? If this seems ridiculous, then why not Finland? Norway? Sweden? These all extend directly above Moscow. If these interpreters will not interpret within Ezekiel's geographical frame of reference, demanding a "more literal" understanding of "farthest north," then their own hermeneutic demands they go farther north than Moscow. Their own argument falls."[21] Since Togarmah is said to reside in the "remote north" then there is no need to differentiate from "remote north" or "remotest north" since they mean the same thing. "An examination of the Hebrew text, however, will reveal that these three phrases are essentially the same (there is no need for the differentiation of the adjectives "remote" and "remotest")."[22] This is why the New International Version translates "remote" and "remotest" north as simply the "far north." Therefore, "Scriptural terminology must not be forced into a twentieth-century A.D. map. To Ezekiel the "farthest north" was Asia Minor (from there you jump off the edge!). To extend Ezekiel's frame of reference any further, without exegetical warrant, cannot be right."[23]

In the Last Days

In Ezekiel 38:8 and again in 38:16, Ezekiel gives the time frame for the Battle of Gog and Magog to occur. In 38:8 and in 38:16 Ezekiel uses the terms "latter days" and "last days" respectively and because of this we are told and led to believe that this battle "will occur in the final time of history in preparation for the establishment of the messianic kingdom of Christ."[24] There are scholars that disagree with how modern day prophecy writers deal with these terms in Ezekiel 38.

One such scholar is J. A. Thompson who states in his commentary on Deuteronomy, where the same phrase "latter days" used in Ezekiel 38:16 is also used in Deuteronomy 4:30. "The phrase *in the latter days* need not be interpreted eschatologically, but merely in the sense of 'in the future.'"[25] The phrase in the latter days "actually points to an occasion in the future which takes place at the end of a certain but indefinitely defined length of time. This can be clearly seen in Num 24:14—"I shall counsel you what this people will do to your people at the end of days." Balaam is obviously referring to a future event involving Moab and Israel, and not to the ultimate end of all time."[26] The Hebrew language does not have a phrase equivalent to the English phrases "in the future" or "in the past". There are simply "days ahead" or "latter days" (Deut. 4:30) or there are "former days" (Deut. 4:32).[27]

Even Joel Rosenberg, whose book *Epicenter* interprets the events of Ezekiel 38 and 39 as still yet future, agrees with this analysis. He states, "Ezekiel 38:16 does say these events will happen in the "last days" (NASB), but this term is not necessarily limited to the period of the Tribulation ...It's important to note that the Hebrew term translated as "the last days" can also be translated as "in the distant future"(NLT) or "in days to come" (NIV)."[28] The expression 'in the latter days" "is an expression frequently used in Biblical prophecy, pointing to the final part of whatever period of history the prophet has in view. Thus Jacob used the term "last days" in reference to the ultimate fortune of each of the twelve tribes in the land of Canaan (Gen. 49:1); Balaam applied the term to the first advent of Christ (Num. 24:14); Moses used it in a generally sense of the distant future, when Israel would experience tribulation (Deut. 4:30)."[29]

God promised to restore the fortunes of both Moab in Elam *"in the latter days"* (Jeremiah. 48:47; 49:39). This is the exact same phrase found in Ezekiel 38:8 and 38:16. We find the fulfillment of this restoration in the book of Acts where those that participated in Pentecost where the "Parthians, Medes and *Elamites*; residents of Mesopotamia, Judea and Cappadocia, Pontus and Asia, Phrygia and Pamphylia, Egypt along with and the parts of Libya near Cyrene; visitors from Rome both Jews and converts to Judaism Cretans and Arabs" (Acts 2:9-11). These nations at Pentecost represented nations from "every nation under heaven" (Acts 2:5) and would have included those from Moab. Clearly, the restored fortunes of Elam and Moab where fulfilled *"in the latter days"* or in *"the last days"*, the New Testament era, just as Jeremiah had prophesied.[30]

The phrase "in the latter days" is also found in Daniel 2:28 and again in 10:14. The events prophesied in Daniel 2 were fulfilled in the future when the Babylonians were conquered by the Medo-Persian Empire (Daniel 5:25-31, cf.2:39; 7:5), who were eventually conquered by Alexander and the Greeks (Daniel 8:3-8, cf.2:39; 7:6), who in turn was conquered by the Romans the fourth kingdom in Nebuchadnezzar's dream (Daniel 2:40-43; 7:7-8). This was the ruling power during the ministry of Jesus and when the New Testament was written (Luke 2:1; 20:25; Acts 11:28; 18:2; 27:24).

A literal interpretation of these phrases does mean that this is a reference to some eschatological event in the distant future near the end of human history. These phrases used by Ezekiel are consistent with their uses in other passages in the Bible that are describing events that would happen in his future. "There is no reason to skip over all of history and nearly 2000 years of the so called Church age and rework Ezekiel's prophecy so that it fits an end-time scenario that includes unnamed nations fighting with ancient weapons."[31]

Notes

[1] Gary DeMar, *The Fiction Behind Left Behind*, p.13

[2] Gary DeMar, *Zechariah 12 and the "Esther Connection": The Prophetic Fulfillment of the Rescue of Israel* (Powder Springs, GA: American Vision, 2005), p.11

[3] Gary DeMar, *Why the End of the World is Not in Your Future: Identifying the Gog-Magog Alliance* (Powder Springs, GA: American Vision Press, 2008), p.94

[4] John MacArthur, "Jeremiah" *The MacArthur Bible Commentary* (Nashville, TN: Thomas Nelson, 2005), p.844

[5] Dwight Wilson, *Armageddon Now!: The Premillenarian Response to Russia and Israel Since 1917* (Tyler, TX: Institute for Christian Economics, [1977] 1991), p.68

[6] ibid, p.125

[7] Mark Hitchcock and Thomas Ice, *The Truth Behind Left Behind: A Biblical View of the End Times* (Sisters, OR: Multnomah Press, 2004), p.61-72

[8] ibid, p.61-62

[9] John F. Walvoord, *Israel In Prophecy* (Grand Rapids, MI: Zondervan, 1962), p.108

[10] J.A. Thompson, *Deuteronomy*, Tyndale Old Testament Commentaries (Downer Grove, IL: InterVarsity Press, 1974), p.284-285

[11] Peter C. Craigie, *The Book of Deuteronomy*, NICOT, (Grand Rapids, MI: Eerdmans, 1976), p.363

[12] http://www.cc-vw.org/articles/debate.html

[13] John Hagee, *Beginning Of The End: The Assassination of Yitzhak Rabin and the Coming of Antichrist* (Nashville, TN: Thomas Nelson, 1996), p.93

[14] Mark Hitchcock, *After the Empire* (Wheaton, Ill: Tyndale House, 1994), p.63

[15] David Chilton, *The Great Tribulation*, (Fort Worth, TX: Institute for Christian Economics, [1987], 1997), p.111

[16] Charles H. Dyer, "Jeremiah", *The Bible Knowledge Commentary: Old Testament*, eds. John F. Walvoord and Roy B. Zuck (Wheaton, IL: Victor Books, 1985), p.1139. ©1985 Cook Communications Ministries. *Bible Knowledge Commentary: Old Testament* by Walvoord and Zuck. Used with permission. May not be further reproduced. All rights reserved.

[17] ibid, p.1135

[18] Timothy J. Dailey, *The Gathering Storm* (Tarrytown, NY: Fleming H. Revell, 1992), p.166

[19] *Zondvervan NIV Study Bible*, "Isaiah," ed. Kenneth L. Barker (Grand Rapids, MI: Zondervan, 2002), p.1090

[20] J. Paul Tanner, "Rethinking Ezekiel's Invasion of Gog," *Journal of the Evangelical Theological Society* 39:1 (March 1996), p.35

[21] Fred G. Zaspel, "The Nations of Ezekiel 38 – 39: Who Will Participate in the Battle?" (1985): http://www.biblical-studies.com/bstudy/eschatology/ezekiel.htm

[22] J. Paul Tanner, "Rethinking Ezekiel's Invasion of Gog," *Journal of the Evangelical Theological Society*, p.33

[23] Fred G. Zaspel, "The Nations of Ezekiel 38 – 39: Who Will Participate in the Battle?"

[24] Mark Hitchcock and Thomas Ice, *The Truth Behind Left Behind: A Biblical View of the End Times* (Sisters OR: Multnomah Publishers, 2004), p.90

[25] J .A. Thompson, *"Deuteronomy,* p.108

[26] John R. Wilch, Time and Event: *An Exegetical Study of the Use of 'ēth in the Old Testament in Comparison to Other Temporal Expressions in Clarification of the Concept of Time* (Atlanta, GA: Society of Biblical Literature, 1970), p.69

[27] Peter C. Craigie, *The Book of Deuteronomy*, p.141

[28] Joel C. Rosenberg, *Epicenter: Why the Current Rumblings in the Middle East Will Change Your Future* (Carol Stream, IL: Tyndale House, 2006), p.252

[29] *Commentary on Daniel and Revelation*, "Daniel" (Hagerstown, MD: Review & Herald Publishing, 2008), p.861

[30] Gary DeMar, *Why the End of the World is Not in Your Future*, p.92

[31] ibid, p.91

CHAPTER EIGHT

The Fulfillment of Ezekiel 38 & 39

—∿—

ontemporary prophecy writers often claim that Ezekiel was able to look down the corridors of time and was given the ability to prophesy about events that would happen in our day. They often write, "The Hebrew prophet Ezekiel, writing from captivity in Babylon over 2,500 years ago, foretold the rise of a great military alliance "in the latter times" that would mount an invasion force against Israel. The alliance will be led by Gog [modern Russia] together with Persia [modern Iran] which includes most Muslim nations of the Middle East and North Africa."[1] According to these writers, Ezekiel was given such great foresight by God that he was "able to look down the corridors of time and see nations not yet born, and alliances not yet formed. In doing so, he foretold the rise of a Russian military alliance with Iran and other Middle Eastern countries to annihilate Israel during the earth's "last days."[2]

The problem with this view is that it allows prophecy writers to always claim that the events of Ezekiel 38 and 39 are still future. As long as the geo-political landscape changes (and it always does) modern day prophecy writers will never have to deal with its actual fulfillment. They never have to go out on a limb and put their reputations on the line. Instead they just change the outline of their books and show how today's headlines are somehow fulfilling Bible prophecy. It's an easy out.

However, there are individuals, James B. Jordan and Gary DeMar to be precise, who are putting their reputations on the line and are dealing with the difficult passages of Ezekiel 38 and 39 and its historical fulfillment found within the pages of the Bible instead of the newspaper headlines.

Haman is Gog

In chapter seven, I stipulated that Haman was the person that fulfills the role of Gog in Ezekiel 38 and 39. Gary DeMar, who first discussed this in his book *Last Days Madness* released in 1999, introduced me to this interpretation. He discussed it again in his book *End Times Fiction* which was a critique of the *Left Behind* theology and finally did an in depth analysis of the Haman/Gog connection in his latest book on prophecy *Why the End of the World in Not in Your Future*. In spite of the criticism leveled against this interpretation, there is a lot of merit to it especially since it is not dependent on today's newspaper headlines and etymology. A biblical case can be made that the invader being prophesied about in Ezekiel 38 and 39 is none other than the infamous and evil Haman.

Critics of the Haman/Gog interpretation claim that the events described in the book of Esther do not fulfill Ezekiel 38 and 39 because "No invasion on the magnitude of Ezekiel 38-39 has ever taken place in Israel's history."[3] However, a critical study of these passages, and letting scripture interpret scripture, there enough parallels between Ezekiel 38 and 39 with the book of Esther that it should not be dismissed in a cavalier fashion.

Ezekiel 38:1-4 and 39:1 says that Gog is the chief prince of Meshech, Tubal, Gomer, Beth Togarmah, Put and Cush and Haman would most certainly qualify. In Esther chapter three, Ahasuerus promoted Haman to a position that made him second in rank only to the king (Esther 3:1-4; 5:11; cf. 8:2; 10:3). Esther 3:1-2, 12 describes Haman as being the leader over the king's satraps, governors, princes, and nobles of the various provinces of the Persian Empire. His promotion "raised him to the rank of vizier, or prime confidential minister, whose pre-eminence in office and power"[4] allowed him to be called the chief prince, of the Persian Empire. Haman is also identified with one of Israel's mortal enemies the Amalekites. In his commentary on the book of Esther, Lewis Bayles Paton on the Haman/Agag/Amalek connection writes:

"The only Agag mentioned in the OT is the King of Amalek [Num. 24:7; 1 Sam. 15:9]... [A]ll Jewish, and many Christian [commentators] think that Haman is meant to be a descendant of this Agag. This view is probably correct, because Mordecai, his rival, is a descendant of Saul ben Kish, who overthrew Agag [1 Sam. 17:8-16]. Amalek was the most ancient foe of Israel [Exod. 17: 10-16] and is specially cursed in the Law [Deut. 25:17]. It is, therefore, probably the author's intention to represent Haman as descended from this race that was characterized by an ancient and unquenchable hatred of Israel *(cf. Esther* 3:10, "he enemy of the Jews")."[5]

"Haman, the chief antagonist, is introduced as an Agagite. Agag was the Amalekite king who was the cause of Saul's downfall (1 Sam.15:8-33). Further, the Amalekites were hereditary enemies of Israel (Exod. 17:8-16; Num. 24:20). Thus, Haman and Mordecai (a Jew and a kinsman of Saul) are natural antagonists. Haman's promotion does not bode well for the Jews."[6] The tension that we see between Haman (the Amalekite) and Mordecai (the Jew) was an age old struggle between these two nations that finally culminates in the events of Ezekiel and Esther.

Ezekiel 38:5-6 states that Gog, the chief prince, will be leading military forces that stretch literally from Persia to Ethiopia (Cush). "He is the commander-in-chief ($n^e \acute{s}\hat{\imath}$' $r\bar{o}$'$\hat{s}$ [chief prince]) of a coalition of forces gathered from the ends of the earth. He himself is from the land of Magog, and he rules over Meshech-Tubal. His allies include Persia, Cush, and Put (38:5), along with Gomer and Beth Togermah (38:6). It is no coincidence that together these make up a total of seven nations, and it is significant that they are gathered from the uttermost parts of the world known to the prophet. Meshech-Tubal, Gomer and Beth Togermah come from the north, Put (northwest Egypt), and Cush (southern Egypt) from the south and west, while Persia is to the East of Judah."[7] As I showed in chapter seven, Meshech, Tubal, Gomer, Beth Togarmah, Put and Cush fell well within the boundaries of the Persian Empire. The Persian Empire had 127 provinces that stretched from Ethiopia (Cush) to India (see Esther 1:1; 8:9; 9:30).[8] Because Meshech, Tubal, Gomer, Beth Togarmah, Put and Cush were within the boundaries of the Persian Empire, they would have been aligned with the invaders in this invasion against Israel as vassal states of the Persian Empire, with Haman as the leader. Since Meshech, Tubal, Gomer and Beth Togarmah were located in Asia Minor (now modern day Turkey) which is north of Israel; they would have come from the north just as Ezekiel prophesied (38:6, 15; 39:2, also see chapter 8).

In Ezekiel 38:10, the LORD regarding Gog said, "On that day thoughts will come into your mind and you will devise *an evil scheme.*" The book of Esther explains Ezekiel 38:10 and reveals the evil scheme that was devised in Haman's head. In Esther chapter three, Haman became enraged when

Mordecai would not pay Haman homage and bow down to him: "When Haman saw that Mordecai would not kneel down or pay him honor, he was enraged" (Esther 3:5). "The [Septuagint] and Josephus [*Antiq.* 11.6.5] claim that Haman demanded *divine* honors, which Mordecai as a Jew could not pay. The targums state that Haman wore an idol pinned to his breast, which would make bowing by Mordecai idolatry."[9] Because Mordecai would not bow down and pay homage to Haman, Haman decided that he would not only kill Mordecai but also all of the Jews throughout the Persian Empire: "Yet having learned who Mordecai's people were, he scorned the idea of killing only Mordecai. Instead Haman looked for a way to destroy all Mordecai's people, the Jews, throughout the whole kingdom of Xerxes" (Esther 3:6, see also verses 8-13). This would have included the Jews that had returned to the land of Israel. Upon learning of the plot by Haman to destroy the Jews, Esther went before the Ahasuerus "and begged him to put an end to *the evil plan* of Haman the Agagite, which he had devised against the Jews" (Esther 8:3; 9:25; cf. Ezekiel 38:10).

The Land of Desolation and Unwalled Villages

Ezekiel 38:8-11 says that the enemies of Israel would invade a land of "unwalled villages - without walls and without gates and bars- that had recovered from war and whose people had been gathered from many nations to a land that had been long desolate." In typical fashion, modern prophecy writers take Ezekiel's words in this passage and try to apply them to today's realities. This is exactly what Grant Jeffrey does in his book *The Next World War*:

> "It is interesting to note that during the lifetime of Ezekiel and up until 1900, virtually all of the villages and cities in the Middle East had walls for defense. Ezekiel had never seen a village or city without defensive walls. Yet, in our day, Israel is a "land of unwalled villages" for the simple reason that modern techniques of warfare (bombs and missiles) make city walls irrelevant for defense. This is one more indication that his prophecy refers to our modern generation."[10]

He continues on, writing, "Ezekiel's reference to "dwell safely" and "without walls . . . neither bars nor gates" refers precisely to Israel's current military situation, where she is dwelling safely because of her strong armed defense and where her cities and villages have no walls or defensive bars. The prophet had never seen a city without walls, so he was astonished when he saw, in a vision, Israel dwelling in the future without walls. Ezekiel lived in a time when every city in the world used huge walls for military defense."[11]

This is sheer nonsense and a good example of how modern prophecy writers will go to any lengths to prove how modern day events are somehow fulfilling Bible prophecy. It is sheer nonsense for a couple of reasons. First off, Israel today is not without defensive walls. Israel began building a series of large defensive walls along the Green Line that divides Israel from the West Bank.[12] According to the *Jerusalem Post*, to date, Israel has built some 280 miles of the planned 490 miles of defensive walls that the Israeli government expects to be completed sometime in 2010.[13] They have been credited with the decreasing the number of homicide bombers targeting Israel.[14]

Secondly, even though Israel's defensive wall has been credited with decreasing the number homicide bomber attacks, today Israel does not live in safety and peace as outlined in Ezekiel 38 and 39. Although defensive walls were great defensive measures during wars fought in antiquity, Israel's defensive walls today has not given it the peace and security that it desires. Israel's vulnerability was on clear display in its forty-day war with Hezbollah during the summer of 2006. Israel was under constant aerial bombardment of rockets raining down from Lebanon. Israel's defensive walls are an impotent defensive measure against modern military offensive weapons like missiles, bombs and intercontinental ballistic missiles, which Iran is threatening to use against Israel on a regular basis.

As Gary DeMar has commented, it is "In Esther 9:19 we learn that there were Jews who were living peacefully in "unwalled towns" (KJV) when Haman conspired against them. Israel's antagonists in Ezekiel are said to "go up against the land of unwalled villages" (38:11). The Hebrew word *perazah* is used in Esther 9:13 and Ezekiel 38:11."[15] The biblical record is clear regarding the walls of Jerusalem. Jerusalem had become an unwalled city after its sacking at the hands of the King Nebuchadnezzar and the Babylonians which "fits the prophetic description of the period in Ezekiel 38:11 and the historical fulfillment of Esther 9:19."[16]

God, through Ezekiel, warned the Israelites that because of their sin of idolatry He was going to "make the land a desolate waste from the desert to Diblah" (Ezekiel 6:14). God, through Ezekiel and Jeremiah consistently warned the

Jews the He was going to desolate the land because of their sin (Ezekiel 12:20; 15:8; 33:27-29; Jeremiah 7:34; 10:22; 12:11; 25:8-11; 33:10). The book of Lamentations confirms God's promise to desolate the land: "for Mount Zion, which lies desolate, with jackals prowling over it" (Lamentation 5:18). The prophet Micah said that Jerusalem was in shambles. It had "become a heap of rubble" with "the temple hill a mound overgrown with thickets" (Micah 3:12). The prophet Zechariah prophesying to the Jews that had returned to Israel from captivity reiterated to them that, "the land was left so desolate" due to their sin of injustice and oppression (Zechariah 7:14).

Regarding the walls of Jerusalem, the book of Lamentations states, "The LORD determined to tear down the wall around the Daughter of Zion...He made ramparts and walls lament; together they wasted away...Her gates have sunk into the ground; their bars he has broken and destroyed" (Lamentations 2:8-9).

According to Josephus, Nebuzaradan, the general of Nebuchadnezzar's army, was ordered to plunder the temple and the palace, and then set fire to the both. He was also to raze the city to the ground and transplant its people to Babylonia.[17] This account of Nebuzaradan's actions by

Josephus is confirmed in the Bible. In II Kings chapter 25 it says, "The whole Babylonian army, under the commander of the imperial guard, <u>broke down the walls around Jerusalem</u>" (II Kings 25:10; also see II Chronicles 36:19).

After the seventy-years of Israel's captivity were completed, Cyrus the king of the Persian Empire issued a decree for the Jews to return to their homeland "in order to fulfill the word of LORD by the mouth of Jeremiah" (Ezra 1:1; II Chronicles 36:22). When Cyrus gave the decree for the exiles to return home, close to 50,000 Jews returned home from the nations that God had exiled them (Nehemiah 7:66; Jeremiah 29:14; Ezekiel 6:8, 9; 12:16) . They returned to the mountains of Israel, which had long been desolate (Lamentation 5:18; Ezekiel 6:14; 12:20) in order to begin rebuilding the temple and the city that Nebuchadnezzar had destroyed (Ezra 2:64; Nehemiah 1:3). It was during this time that they began to restore the walls and the foundations that had been destroyed during the Babylonian siege (Ezra 4:12, 13; Nehemiah 2:8, 11-17; 4:1-10, 13-21; 6:1).

In spite of the decree by Cyrus to rebuild, the attempts at rebuilding what had been destroyed by Nebuchadnezzar were being frustrated by the likes of Sanballat, Tobiah, and Tattenai who was governor of the Trans-Euphrates area.

These men are described as being the enemies of the returning exiles (Nehemiah 6:1). These antagonists leveled an accusation against the returning exiles that insinuated rebellion and revolt (Ezra 4:6, 12; Nehemiah 2:19; 6:5) that would have surely brought the full fury of the Persian Empire against the returning exiles. They even threatened the returning exiles with murder in order to make them afraid enough to frustrate the rebuilding of Jerusalem (Nehemiah 4:4, 11-12). King Darius ultimately responded to these charges that put an end to the hostilities and oppression at the hands of Israel's antagonists allowing the Jews to live in peace and security stated in Ezekiel 38:11 (see Ezra 6:11-12).

Coming to Take a Plunder

In Ezekiel 38:12-13, Israel's enemies are stated to be coming after much plunder. Modern prophecy writers have allegorized what this plunder actually is and twisted the literal meaning in order to fit a modern contemporary setting. For example, Hal Lindsey claimed in his book *The Late Great Planet Earth* that Russia would be enticed to invade Israel because of the mineral wealth found in the Dead Sea. According to Lindsey, prior to Russia's invasion of Israel,

"Israel will become one of the most prosperous nations on earth...a cultural, religious and economic world center, especially at Jerusalem" due to the value of the of the mineral deposits in the Dead Sea that he claims was valued at $1.270 trillion dollars in 1970.[18] With great exuberance, he goes on to claim, "This is more than the combined wealth of France, England, and the United States!"[19]

Joel Rosenberg takes a different stance than Hal Lindsey did in 1970 on what the plunder is that Gog and his confederates are after. In his book *Epicenter,* Rosenberg contends that oil is what will drive Israel's enemies to invade her. Quoting Tim LaHaye, Rosenberg writes, "Suppose that a pool of oil, greater than anything in Arabia...were discovered by the Jews...This would change the course of history. Before long, Israel would be able independently to solve its economic woes, finance the resettlement of the Palestinians, and supply housing for Jews and Arabs in the West Bank, East Bank, or anywhere else they might choose to live. Even if something besides oil were discovered, it would have the same far-reaching effect if it were able to produce high revenues."[20] To ensure that modern prophecy writers are all singing from the same hymnal, Hal Lindsey has changed from what he originally wrote in *The Late Great Planet*

Earth and now agrees with Joel Rosenberg and sees oil as a reason for Russia and Iran to invade Israel. "A massive oil strike in Israel would completely change the balance of power in the Middle East. Such an oil- strike could potentially break the back of OPEC. It is unlikely OPEC would admit Israel as a member, regardless of how much oil she had. That would seem to leave but one option, best expressed by my friend Joel Rosenberg's novel of the same name. The Ezekiel Option."[21] So therefore, "God had supposedly reserved this wealth for the use of His restored people in the twentieth century [now the twenty-first century]"[22] but only for it to be eventually turned over to Israel's enemies after Israel is invaded.

You have to ask yourself; what would Russia gain by invading the tiny nation of Israel? The nation of Israel, according *The World Factbook*, is ranked fifty-fourth amongst exporting nations. In 2006, Israeli exports reached $42.86 billion[23] and in 2008, it reached $54.16 billion.[24] Israel's chief exports are machinery and equipment, software, cut diamonds, agricultural products (fruits and vegetables), chemicals, textiles and apparel. Noticeably missing from that list are livestock and commodities like gold, silver (Ezekiel 38:12-13) and oil. Its economy depends on imports of crude oil, grains, raw materials, and especially military equipment from the United States.[25] Peter and Patti Lalonde wrote in their book *The Edge of Time* that, "Russia possesses more natural resources than any other nation in the world. It holds 13% of the world's crude oil, 35% of the world's natural gas resources, 12% of the world's coal supply, 32% of its iron ore, 27% of its tin, and 11%of the world's copper resources."[26]

According to the CIA's *The World Factbook*, Russia has the world's largest natural gas reserves, the second largest coal reserves and the eighth largest oil reserves. It is the world's leading natural gas exporter and the second leading oil exporter. Oil, natural gas, metals, and timber account for more than 80% of Russian exports abroad ranking them eighth amongst the world's leading exporting nations.[27]

Statistics published by the oil cartel OPEC in 2006 showed that Russia at the time was extracting more oil than Saudi Arabia, making it the biggest producer of "black gold" in the world. OPEC statistics showed that in the period since 2002 Russian companies have surpassed the Saudis as the world's biggest oil producers on an on-and-off basis. According to OPEC, in June 2006, Russia extracted 9.236 million barrels of oil, which is 46,000 barrels more than Saudi Arabia.[28] As if that were not enough Russia has now laid claim to the oil rich regions of the Arctic.[29] Israel on the other hand does not even rank in the top 50. They are in the very bottom of nations with proven oil reserves ahead of only Barbados, Jordan and Spain, and behind countries like the Czech Republic.[30] It seems obvious that if oil were the enticement for Russia to invade Israel as modern prophecy writers are now claiming, the proven reserves of oil rich countries like Iran, Iraq, and Saudi Arabia would be more enticing. If oil were truly the impetus for an invasion, the countries with the largest proven oil reserves such as Saudi Arabia, Canada, Iran, Iraq, United Arab Emirates, Kuwait, and Venezuela would be at the head of Russia's list of nations to invade and not Israel. Israel simply does not offer Russia much of a reason to invade her it would be a complete waste of time. Not even Israel's gold reserves would be enough to entice Russia. "Russia has gold reserves of nearly $40 billion. This puts them in the top ten worldwide. As compared to other nations, Israel does not make the top twenty list."[31]

Mark Hitchcock, in his book *The Coming Islamic Invasion of Israel*, says that one reason for the attack against Israel by the invading coalition "is to come against the Antichrist and the Western World."[32] Where does it say anything remotely close to that in Ezekiel 38 and 39?! Ezekiel 38:12-13 states exactly who Israel's enemies are and what they are coming after. If taken in a literal fashion, like the weapons that are listed in Ezekiel 38:4, 15 and 39:3, 9, the text literal means what it says. There is no need to insert a person that the text does not mention at all or to allegorize livestock, gold and silver into minerals, potash, or crude oil. Ezekiel 38:13 makes it clear that the invaders are coming for silver, gold, livestock, and goods. The plunder that they were coming after is the very same items that are listed in Ezra.

In Ezra when Cyrus gave the decree for the Jews to return home "the survivors were to be provided with gold, silver, with goods and livestock" (Ezra 1:4). Ezra continues by saying that "All their neighbors assisted them with articles of silver and gold, with goods and livestock, and with valuable gifts" (Ezra 1:6, see vv 7-11). Upon the return of the exiles, some of these items were put into the treasury in Jerusalem (Ezra 2:68). Darius and Artaxerxes issued similar decrees to the one Cyrus gave ordering that those returning to Israel were to be supplied with silver, gold, livestock, and goods. The very same items listed in Ezekiel 38:13, with some of these items going into the temple treasury (Ezra 6:5, 9; 7:15-20; cf. Ezra 8:25-28; Nehemiah 7:71-72).

When the decree was issued to destroy the Jews, Haman said that he would put "ten thousand talents of silver into the royal treasury for the men who carry out this business" (Esther 3:9; cf. 4:7). In verse eleven Haman is told by the king to keep his money. So where would the money come from? It would come from the exiles that were returning home. "Keep the money," the king said to Haman, "and do with the people as you please" (Ezra 3:11). The Gog/Magog invaders were going to take the plunder from the invasion as payment for their services that were rendered to the cause of Haman.

Russia's Broken Military

The financial resources that would be needed for Russia to invade Israel would be staggering. World military expenditure in 2007 is estimated to have reached $1.339 trillion in current dollars. This represents a 6 percent increase in real terms since 2006 and a 45 percent increase over the 10-year period since 1998. The United States is responsible for about 80% of the increase in 2005 with its military expenditure now accounting for just under half of the world total, at 45% and is distantly followed by the UK, China, France, and Japan each with 4 to 5 percent of the world's share.[33]

For example, The Center for Arms Control and Non-Proliferation puts the cost of the wars in Iraq and Afghanistan at approximately $872 billion.[34] In December 2008, U.S. News & World Report put the cost of the wars at slightly over $900 billion at $904 billion since 2001.[35] A comparison of the military budgets of the U.S. and Russia show an incredible disparity between the two nations. "The U.S. budget for 1999 was almost $280 billion while the Kremlin Russian budget was just a fraction of that, at an estimated $5.6 billion. Back in the Soviet days, Moscow gave the lion's share of its resources to the armed forces—in the 1980s — about $200 billion a year, experts say."[36]

During Russia's second military showdown with the breakaway republic of Chechnya, Russia saw its military budget plummet by about 75% from Soviet-era spending levels, to around $4 billion, which at the time was less than 3% of the country's total gross domestic product. In 2005, the Russian military budget for spending and defense appropriations rose to $18 billion up 22% from 2004's budget of $14 billion and in 2006 it rose 27% to $24.9 and by 2007 Russia had seen its budget quadruple to $31 billion from the previous six years. Currently Russia is spending between 2.6% and 2.9% of its GDP and will see its military budget grow to $50 billion for 2009.[37] Even with this increase in spending, it represents roughly only 5.5% of what the United States has spent on the invasions of Iraq and Afghanistan and is roughly 7.6% of the United States' $651.2 billion dollar military budget for FY2009, which is 4.7% of its GDP.

Budgetary issues are not the only thing plaguing the Russian military. Russia's military is seriously struggling with the inadequate training of conscripts, a flagging morale, soaring suicide rates in the army, rampant draft evasion, paratroopers that are refusing to fight altogether, and getting away with it, cash-strapped officers and soldiers increasingly moonlighting to supplement their meager salaries, and an alarming drop in the number of junior officers with battle expertise. According to Mark Galeotti, a Russian military analyst at Keele University in Britain "What we are seeing is an across-the-board decay." He believes it is misleading to say Russia's army consists of 1.2 million conscripts - down from 2.8 million in 1992 and around 5 million at the height of the Soviet period. "What proportion of these soldiers can really fight?" he asks. "I think the Russian forces in reality are no more than 200,000 in terms of how we would genuinely assess [their battle preparedness]."[38]

In a September 8, 2000 BBC article, it stated, "Russia is to cut its armed forces by almost a third, a reduction of about 350,000, from its current strength of 1.2 million. The BBC article went on to say that these measures "are being seen as recognition by the government that the country can no longer afford the huge armed forces it boasted during the Soviet era."[39] According to these numbers, that would leave Russia with a fighting force of only 850,000 troops.

There are further examples of Russian military decay. In January 2002 "Russian defence systems faced a crisis when power supplies were cut to a centre monitoring military satellites...The black-out of computers at the centre on the far eastern Kamchatka Peninsula happened when the local power company, Kamchatenergo, pulled the plug because of unpaid bills. It is the latest incident in which power companies have lost patience with the Russian military for failing to pay its bills."[40] In February 2004, during military exercises attended by Russian President Vladimir Putin, "A Russian ballistic missile...fired from submarine Karelia, was blown up by its automatic safety system, after veering from its flight path."[41] Just the day before two ballistic missiles failed to launch from the Novomosskovsk submarine. The missiles had been due to take off from the nuclear submarine, the

Novomosskovsk, with Mr. Putin watching from another submarine, the Arkhangelsk.[42]

Among American defense planners, there is a belief that the vast majority of the Russian nuclear defense program is nearing the end of its reliable lifecycle, and that replacing the entire fleet would be well beyond Russia's financial capacity. From the U.S. point of view, there is no reason to subject itself to a new treaty that would limit U.S. options, particularly when the Russia of today is far less able to support an arms race than the Soviet Union of yesteryear.[43] In 2007, the BBC reported how young army conscripts were forced to work as male prostitutes by the older service men.[44] A New Yorker article summed up well the current state of the Russian military when it stated:

"The Russian Army, the inheritor of the structures, arms, and tactics of the Soviet armed forces, is now a shambles: a psychological wreck, a material ruin. Conscription is still universal, but only notionally so. It's easy to bribe your way out of the draft for a couple of thousand dollars. It is only the least skilled, the least educated, who enlist. Many of the draftees are illiterate and in such poor physical condition that they are useless as anything more than cannon fodder in Chechnya or as sources of abuse for their predatory superiors. *Dyedovshchina*, the sadistic, often fatal, hazing of recruits, is ubiquitous: soldiers are routinely humiliated and tortured by their commanders, beaten with sticks, chains, chairs, anything at hand. Every year, thousands are wounded and hundreds are killed or commit suicide; thousands more go awol as a result of the abuse. The Russian Army is preposterously top-heavy-there are five times the number of generals as in the American armed services-and, for many of those officers and commanders, life has been so leeched of a sense of mission and pride that they destroy themselves with drink; their salaries are so low that they ease into a life of corruption, petty or grand."[45]

Russia's Broken Military

Russia's military is not the only thing that is broken. So is the Russian economy. Russia has been hit hard with the downturn in the worldwide economy. At the beginning of the downturn, Russia saw its stock market crash in one day by 17% in a broad based selloff that caused trading on the stock market to be halted.[46] In the first quarter of 2009, Russia's economy had shrunk by over 23 percent and Russian President Dmitry

Medvedev expects Russia's economy will shrink more than previously predicted for 2009.[47] Russian economists expect the Russian economy to continue to decline until 2011 and they expect to see only extremely modest GDP growth.[48]

According to Dr. Doom Nouriel Roubini, since the downturn in the economy Russia, "has experienced a capital flight of over $100 billion and has lost about $150 billion of foreign reserves (now down to about a $450 billion level); it is facing massive external debt financing problems as its banks financed their lending with foreign currency borrowings and its corporate firms financed massive expansion with foreign currency debt; it is now desperately trying to prevent a sharp depreciation of its currency by aggressive forex intervention; it may face a large fiscal deficit (2% of GDP) next year; and its GDP growth rate is sharply slowing down leading the World Bank to predict a growth rate of 3% alone in 2009 while leading local analysts are predicting an actual recession (negative growth of as much as -2%) in 2009."[49] Russia has also had its credit rating dropped by S&P from "BBB+ to BBB because of the "rapid depletion" of the country's foreign exchange reserves and the "difficulty of meeting the country's external financing needs.""[50]

Russia is also seeing a massive decline in its population of 141 million citizens due to low birth rates and high death rates; a trend that has been taking place since the early 1990's and is directly attributed to alcoholism, suicide, and especially HIV/AIDS. According to the Global Fund for to Fight AIDS, between 900,000 and one million people in Russia have the HIV virus, while Russian experts say the true number of HIV-positive cases in Russia is close to 1.3 million.[51] This dramatic decrease in the Russian population is prompting Russia "to reverse a trend in which the population is shrinking by about 700,000 people a year as births fail to outpace a high death rate boosted by AIDS, alcoholism and suicide."[52] This trend has lead to the governor of a central Russian province, Sergei Morozov, to encourage couples to take time off from work to procreate.[53]

In light of all this, it seems highly unlikely that Russia would be interested in invading Israel. Based on the condition of the Russian military, Russia could not mount the type of operation needed to invade the country of Israel whose military forces are in far better shape than their Russian counterparts. Finally, given the condition of the Russian economy and its declining population, Russia could not sustain a military invasion because of the financial hardship that it would place on an already very weak economy and declining population.

Torrents of Hailstones, Sulfur and Fire

Modern prophecy writers have often interpreted the destruction of Gog and his confederates in light of today's modern military instruments of warfare. Ezekiel 39:6 says fire will be sent on Magog and the coastland. "I will send fire on Magog and on those who live in safety in the coastlands, and they will know that I am the LORD." Some of today's prophecy writers associate the destruction of Gog/Magog as a description consistent with that of a nuclear conflagration. This was the position of Zola Levitt and Thomas McCall in their co-authored book *The Coming Russian Invasion of Israel.* "The fire falling upon a land army is not nearly as difficult to imagine in this age as it was in Ezekiel's time. Napalm or even nuclear detonations might well be described in this way."[54] But even they admit that this speculative. This is also the same position taken up by John Hagee in *Jerusalem Countdown.* He believes that the language describing fiery destruction on the coastlands "could describe a nuclear war via an exchange of nuclear missiles."[55] Joel Rosenberg like Hagee interprets Ezekiel 39:6 in the following way:

"This suggests that targets throughout Russia and the former Soviet Union, as well as Russia's allies, will be supernaturally struck on this day of judgment and partially or completely consumed. These could be limited to nuclear missile silos, military bases, radar installations, defense ministries, intelligence headquarters, and other government buildings of various kinds. But such targets could very well also include religious centers, such as mosques, madrassas, Islamic schools and universities, and other facilities that preach hatred against Jews and Christians and call for the destruction of Israel. Either way, we will have to expect extensive collateral damage, and many civilians will be at severe risk."[56]

Other modern day prophecy writers take a different approach and argue for a more literal interpretation. They see the destruction of the invading forces as a supernatural intervention of God from heaven. In order to maintain a literal interpretation they argue, "The invaders are destroyed by a massive earthquake in the land of Israel, infighting, plagues, and fire from heaven (38:19-22). God destroys the enemies supernaturally."[57]

A more plausible interpretation is that Ezekiel like other prophets in the Old Testament is using apocalyptic language that is often employed throughout the Old Testament. This is Gary DeMar's bone of contention with modern day prophecy writers because they "do not take into account how the prophets describe prophetic events and how prophetic language is often different from the actual historical record."[58] He goes on to say, "The decreation language of Ezekiel 38:18-21 is typical of prophetic descriptions of local judgments (see Jer. 4; Zeph. 1:2-4, 18; Joel 3:16; Nahum 1:5-6; Haggai 2:6, 20-23)."[59] As an example, he uses the historical account of David's deliverance from Saul in II Samuel to David's poetic description of the same event in Psalms 18:

"Consider the following and compare these phrases with what actually took place historically in David's battles with Saul and the use of similar language in Ezekiel 38-39:

- "The land shook and quaked" (2 Sam. 22:8; cf. Ps. 18:7; Ezek. 38:19).

- "The foundations of the mountains were trembling and were shaken, because He was angry; (Ps. 18:7b; Ezek. 38:18).

- "He sent out arrows, and scattered them, lightning, and routed them" (2 Sam. 22:15; cf. 18:4)

- "From the brightness before Him passed His thick clouds, hailstones and coals of fire" (Ps. 18:12; Ezek. 38:22).

- "The channels of the sea appeared, the foundations of the world were laid bare, by the rebuke of the LORD, at the blast of the breath of His nostrils" (2 Sam. 22:16; cf. Ps. 18:15; Ezek. 38:20)."[60]

Ezekiel 38:20 says, "The mountains will be overturned, the cliffs will crumble and every wall will fall to the ground." The language of Ezekiel 38:20 is very similar to that of Isaiah 40:4 where we are told that the "rough ground shall become level" and "the rugged places a plain." The language of Isaiah 40:4 is used by the New Testament writers and applied to John the Baptists' preparing the way for the coming of the Messiah (Matthew 3:1-4; Mark 1:3-8; Luke 3:4-6; cf. Isaiah 40:4; Revelation 6:14; 16:20). The language of Ezekiel 38:21-23 is very similar to that of Ezekiel 13:10-

13. In Ezekiel 38:21-23 where God said He "will pour down torrents of rain, hailstones and burning sulfur" on Gog and his confederates, the very same language is being used in Ezekiel 13:10-13 against the false prophets in Israel who would experience the violent thunderstorm of God's divine wrath:

"Because they lead my people astray, saying, "Peace," when there is no peace, and because, when a flimsy wall is built, they cover it with whitewash, therefore tell those who cover it with whitewash that it is going to fall. Rain will come in torrents, and <u>I will send hailstones hurtling down</u>, and violent winds will burst forth. When the wall collapses, will people not ask you, "Where is the whitewash you covered it with?" "Therefore this is what the Sovereign LORD says: In my wrath I will unleash a violent wind, and in my anger <u>hailstones and torrents of rain will fall with destructive fury</u>" (Ezekiel 13:10-13).

Comparing Scripture w/Scripture			
Ezekiel 38:18-20	**Isaiah 40:3-4**	**Micah 1:3-4**	**2 Samuel 22:7-8**
This is what will happen in that day: When Gog attacks the land of Israel, my hot anger will be aroused, declares the Sovereign LORD. In my zeal and fiery wrath I declare that at that time there shall be a great earthquake in the land of Israel. The fish of the sea, the birds of the air, the beasts of the field, every creature that moves along the ground, and all the people on the face of the earth will tremble at my presence. The mountains will be overturned, the cliffs will crumble and every wall will fall to the ground.	A voice of one calling: "In the desert prepare the way for the LORD; make straight in the wilderness a highway for our God. Every valley shall be raised up, every mountain and hill made low; the rough ground shall become level, the rugged places a plain.	Judgment Against Samaria and Jerusalem Look! The LORD is coming from his dwelling place; he comes down and treads the high places of the earth. The mountains melt beneath him and the valleys split apart, like wax before the fire, like water rushing down a slope.	In my distress I called to the LORD; I called out to my God. From his temple he heard my voice; my cry came to his ears. "The earth trembled and quaked, the foundations of the heavens [c] shook: they trembled because he was angry.

Ezekiel 38:21-23		**Isaiah 30:33**	**2 Samuel 22:8-9**
...will summon a sword against Gog on all my mountains, declares the Sovereign LORD. Every man's sword will be against his brother. I will execute judgment upon him with plague and bloodshed; I will pour down torrents of rain, hailstones and burning sulfur on him and on his troops and on the many nations with him. And so I will show my greatness and my holiness, and I will make myself known in the sight of many nations. Then they will know that I am the LORD.'		"Topheth has long been prepared: It has been made ready for the king. Its fire pit has been made deep and wide, with an abundance of fire and wood; the breath of the LORD, like a stream of burning sulfur, sets it ablaze	"The earth trembled and quaked, the foundations of the heavens [c] shook; they trembled because he was angry. Smoke rose from his nostrils; consuming fire came from his mouth, burning coals blazed out of it.

Ezekiel, as a prophet, is doing what prophets before and after him have done. He is using metaphoric language to describe destruction of the enemies of God. This language is closely related to God's wrath, judgment, and destruction. He is describing events from a God-centered perspective while Esther on the other hand is describing events from a man-centered perspective. These are examples in the Old Testament where language like this is used when God destroys His enemies and the enemies of His people.

Notes

[1] Hal Lindsey, "Islam's most reliable ally," *WorldNetDaily* (December 16, 2005): http://www.wnd.com/index.php/index.php?pageId=33932

[2] Joel Rosenberg, "The 'War of Gog and Magog': Understanding Ezekiel 38-39": http://tinyurl.com/yaqm7yv

[3] Ron *Rhodes, Northern Storm Rising: Russia, Iran, and the Emerging End-Times Military Coalition against Israel* (Eugene, OR: Harvest House, 2008), p.169. also see Mark Hitchcock and Thomas Ice, *The Truth Behind Left Behind: A Biblical View of the End Times* (Sisters, OR: Multnomah Press, 2004), p.44-47

[4] Robert Jamieson, A.R. Fausset, and David Brown, "Esther," *Jamieson, Fausset and Brown's Commentary on the Whole Bible* (Grand Rapids, MI: Zondervan, 1961), p.356

[5] Lewis Bayles Paton, *A Critical and Exegetical Commentary on the book of Esther* (New York: Charles Scribner's Sons, 1908), p.194

[6] *Eerdmans Commentary on the Bible*, "Esther," eds. James D. G. Dunn, John William Rogerson (Grand Rapids, MI: Wm. B. Eerdmans, 2003), p.331

[7] Iain M. Duguid, *Ezekiel: The NIV Application Commentary* (Grand Rapids, MI: Zondervan , 1999), p.448

[8] In Esther 8:9, the royal scribes were summoned to write down Mordecai's orders for the Jews to protect themselves from Haman's plot. These orders were sent "to the satraps, governors and nobles of the 127 provinces stretching from India to Cush." (Esther 8:9)

[9] Eerdmans Commentary on the Bible, "Esther," p.331

[10] Grant R. Jeffrey, *The Next World War: What Prophecy Reveals About Extreme Islam and the West* (Colorado Springs, CO: WaterBrook Press, 2006), p.143

[11] ibid, p.147-148

[12] Joshua Hammer, with Joanna Chen and Dan Ephron "Good Fences Make...," *Newsweek* (June 9, 2003), p.32–33.

[13] Tovah Lazaroff, "Fence to be completed only by 2010", *Jerusalem Post* (July 10, 2007): http://tinyurl.com/ycadgyd

[14] Dion Nissenbaum, "Death toll of Israeli civilians killed by Palestinians hit a low in 2006," *McClatchy Newspapers* (June 14, 2007): http://www.mcclatchydc.com/staff/dion_nissenbaum/story/15469.html

[15] Gary DeMar, "Israel: The Land of *Walled* Cities," *American Vision* (January 30, 2007): http://www.americanvision.org/articlearchive2007/01-30-07.asp

[16] Gary DeMar, Why *the End of the World is Not in Your Future: Identifying the Gog-Magog Alliance* (Powder Springs, GA: American Vision Press, 2008), p.56

[17] Paul L. Maier, *Josephus: The Essential Writings*, (Grand Rapids, MI: Kregel Publications, 1988), p.179

[18] Hal Lindsey, *The Late Great Planet Earth* (Grand Rapids, MI: Zondervan, 1970), p.156

[19] ibid, p.156

[20] Tim Lahaye, *The Coming Peace in the Middle East* (Grand Rapids, MI: Zondervan, 1984), p.105; Quoted in Joel Rosenberg, *Epicenter: Why the Current Rumblings in*

the Middle East Will Change your Future (Carol Stream, IL: Tyndale House, 2006), p.55

[21] Hal Lindsey, "Chavez and the 'Ezekiel Option,'" *WorldNetDaily* (February 02, 2007): http://www.wnd.com/index.php?fa=PAGE.view&pageId=39986

[22] *Evangel*, December 13, 1924, pp.6-7 as Quoted in Dwight Wilson, *Armageddon Now!*, (Tyler, TX: Insitute for Christian Economics, 1991), p.79

[23] "Israel," The World Factbook, *Central Intelligence Agency.* (July 19, 2007):https://www.cia.gov/library/publications/the-world-factbook/geos/IS.html

[24] "Israel," The World Factbook, *Central Intelligence Agency.* (August 7, 2009): https://www.cia.gov/library/publications/the-world-factbook/geos/is.html

[25] ibid

[26] Peter and Patti Lalonde, *The Edge of Time: The Final Countdown Has Begun* (Eugene, OR: Harvest House, 1997), p.225-226

[27] "Russia," The World Factbook, *Central Intelligence Agency.* (July 19, 2007): https://www.cia.gov/library/publications/the-world-factbook/geos/rs.html

[28] "Russia Overtakes Saudi Arabia as World's Leading Oil Producer— OPEC" (August 23, 2006): http://www.mosnews.com/money/2006/08/23/russiaoil.shtml

[29] "Putin's Arctic invasion: Russia lays claim to the North Pole and all its gas, oil, and diamonds": http://tinyurl.com/6bf24w

[30] http://www.nationmaster.com/graph/ene_oil_res-energy-oil-reserves

[31] Gary DeMar, *Islam and Russia in Prophecy,* (Powder Springs, GA: American Vision, 2005), p.12

[32] Mark Hitchcock, *The Coming Islamic Invasion of Israel* (Sisters, OR: Multnomah, 2002), p78

[33] Anup Shah, "World Military Spending," (March 1, 2009): http://www.globalissues.org/article/75/world-military-spending

[34] "Total Iraq and Afghanistan Supplemental War Funding To Date," *The Center for Arms Control and Non-Proliferation* (July 23, 2008): http://tinyurl.com/6gq3ta

[35] Alex Kingsbury, "Cost of Iraq, Afghanistan Wars Tops $900 Billion, Report Finds" *U.S. News & World Report* (December 15, 2008): http://tinyurl.com/5nmxhs

[36] David Ensor, "Accident typifies plight of Russian military," *CNN* (July 9, 2001): http://archives.cnn.com/2000/WORLD/europe/08/19/russia.military/

[37] http://www.globalsecurity.org/military/world/russia/mo-budget.htm

[38] Douglas Herbert, "Sinking a symptom of Russia's military malaise," *CNN* (August 21, 2000): http://archives.cnn.com/2000/WORLD/europe/08/14/russia.military/

[39] "Russia to slash armed forces," *BBC* (September 8, 2000): http://news.bbc.co.uk/2/hi/europe/916297.stm-

[40] "Power cuts hit Russian space centre", *BBC* (January 26, 2002): http://news.bbc.co.uk/2/hi/europe/1783899.stm

[41] "Second Russian missile misfires," *BBC* (February 18, 2004): http://news.bbc.co.uk/2/hi/europe/3499967.stm

[42] "Russia denies failure of missiles," *BBC* (February 17, 2004): http://news.bbc.co.uk/2/hi/europe/3496291.stm

[43] Peter Zeihan, "Russia: What Now?", (Posted July 03, 2006): http://www.stratfor.com/products/premium/read_article. php?id=268572

[44] "Russian soldiers 'used for sex,'" *BBC* (February 13, 2007): http://news.bbc.co.uk/go/pr/fr/-/2/hi/europe/6356707.stm

[45] David Remnick, "POST-IMPERIAL BLUES; Billionaire oligarchs, Chechen suicide bombers, generals nostalgic for empire-and the reign of Vladimir Putin", *New Yorker Magazine* (October 13, 2003) p.78

[46] Rachel Morarjee, "Russia halts trading after 17% drop," *Financial Times* (September 16 2008): http://www.ft.com/cms/s/0/6ff9306c-83f1-11dd-bf00-000077b07658.html

[47] "Medvedev: Russia GDP to fall further than thought," *Associated Press* (May 25, 2009): http://www.chron.com/disp/story.mpl/front/6440144.html

[48] "Russian economy to continue declining till 2011, optimistic experts say," *Pravda* (July 16, 2009): http://english.pravda.ru/business/finance/16-07-2009/108178-russian_economy-0

[49] Nouriel Roubini, "Rouble Trouble in Russia: The Inconsistent Trinity at Work and the Need for a 20-25% Currency Depreciation," (December 8, 2008): http://tinyurl.com/yax74tf

[50] Catherine Belton, "Rouble exodus hits Russia credit rating," Financial Times (December 8 2008): http://tinyurl.com/y9bawkf

[51] "Russia has almost one million HIV-positive people," *Agence France-Presse* (November 26, 2007): http://www.breitbart.com/article.php?id=071126182046. bmapzxof&show_article=1

[52] James Kilner, "Skip work, make babies, says Russian governor" *Reuters* (September 12, 2007): http://news.yahoo.com/s/nm/20070912/od_uk_nm/oukoe_uk_russia_sex_2

[53] "Russians get day off to procreate, then win prizes" *Denver Post* (August 15, 2007): http://www.denverpost.com/portlet/article/html/fragments/print_article.jsp?articleId=6624865&siteId=36

[54] Thomas McCall and Zola Levitt, *The Coming Invasion of Israel* (Chicago, IL: Moody Press, 1974), p.41

[55] John Hagee, *Jerusalem Countdown: A Warning to the World,* (Lake Mary, FL: Frontline 2006), p.114

[56] Joel C. Rosenberg, *Epicenter: Why the Current Rumblings in the Middle East Will Change Your Future* (Carol Stream, IL: Tyndale House, 2006), p.165

[57] Mark Hitchcock and Thomas Ice, *The Truth Behind Left Behind: A Biblical View of the End Times* (Sisters OR: Multnomah Publishers, 2004), p.45

[58] Gary DeMar, *Why the End of the World is Not in Your Future*, p.138

[59] ibid, p.140

[60] ibid, p.138-139

CHAPTER NINE

Conclusion

—⁊⁊—

A very strong case has been made that the Gog/Magog prophecy of Ezekiel 38 and 39 is not a prelude to the end of the world. What is going on in the Middle East are not signs and portends to the coming end of the world and the Second Coming of Jesus Christ. The events of Ezekiel 38 and 39 are fulfilled in the events of Esther and the returning Jewish exiles. There is nothing in the passages of Ezekiel 38 and 39 that points to a Russian invasion of Israel. The evidence used by modern prophecy writers to suggest a Russian invasion of Israel needless to say has been weighed in the balance and found wanting (Daniel 5:25-29).

In order to push the fulfillment of the events outlined in Ezekiel 38 and 39 into the far future, contemporary prophecy writers do what liberal Bible scholars have done to the book of Daniel albeit with a different outcome. Contemporary prophecy writers are late dating the book of Ezekiel, which allows them to project these prophecies way out into the future with no fulfillment in view. When Ezekiel wrote his book in the 6th century B.C., he was writing to the Jews that had been exiled by King Nebuchadnezzar. Ezekiel dated his prophecies precisely. His first prophecy (1:2) came in the fifth year of Jehoiachin's exile (593 B.C.); his last dated prophecy was in 571 B.C. (29:17). Hence, his ministry lasted twenty-two years.[1]

In Ezekiel 24:1, the LORD informs Ezekiel that the siege of Jerusalem had begun and further instructs Ezekiel to record the date, which would have been January 15, 588 B.C. In Ezekiel 33:21-27, a man that had escaped from Jerusalem told Ezekiel that the city had fallen. This message would have reached Ezekiel five months after the destruction of Jerusalem in August 586 B.C. There is simply no evidence within the book of Ezekiel to suggest that his prophetic ministry extended beyond that of 571 B.C. as some prophecy writers are currently claiming. In fact, Ezekiel was more than likely one of the first set of exiles taken to Babylon under King Nebuchadnezzar before the fall of Jerusalem in 586 B.C.[2]

Ezekiel, like the Apostle John, penned his book during a time of "personal exile and national Jewish distress."[3] The broad purpose of the book of Ezekiel was to remind the generation born during the Babylonian exile of the cause of Israel's destruction (chaps 4-24). The coming judgment of the seven Gentile nations Ammon, Moab, Edom, Philistia, Tyre, Sidon, and Egypt at the hands of Babylon (chaps. 25-32) and of the coming future national restoration of Israel that would include the rebuilt city of Jerusalem and a newly rebuilt temple (chaps 33-48).[4]

"The accomplishment of this prophecy was to demonstrate to "the nations" at the time that "the house of Israel went into exile for their iniquity because they acted treacherously against" God (Ezek. 39:23; cp. 38:23). These witnessing nations are described by Ezekiel as Israel's "adversaries" (39:23). Applying the prophecy of Ezekiel 38 and 39 to modern-day nations is contrary to the historical context. No nation today had any part in Israel's exile 2600 years ago."[5] It is against this historical backdrop that we should be interpreting the book of Ezekiel including chapters 38, 39, and 40.

Ezekiel 38 & 39 and the Esther Connection

In Esther 3, Haman is promoted to a position that is over the king's satraps, governors, princes, and nobles of the 127 provinces of the Persian Empire stretching from India to Ethiopia [lit. Cush] (Esther 1:1; 8:9; 9:30; cf. Ezekiel 38:2, 5; 39:1). A position that was second in command only to Ahasuerus who gave Haman his signet ring confirming Haman's position within the Persian Empire as the chief prince of the Persian Empire. This allowed Haman to issue orders on behalf of the king (Esther 3:1-2,10, 12; 8:2; 10:3; cf. Ezekiel 38:2; 39:1). Due to Haman's perceived disrespect by Mordecai's refusal to bow down to him, Haman devised an evil scheme to destroy the Jews throughout the Persian Empire's 127 provinces. This would have certainly included the Jews that had returned to the Promised Land from exile; a scheme that ultimately would come back on Haman's his own head (Esther 3:8-10; 8:3; 9:25; cf. Ezekiel 38:10; 18-23; 39). These orders to destroy the Jews went to the king's satraps, governors, and the nobles throughout the Persian

Empire's 127 provinces in the language of each nationality which would have included the governor of the Trans Euphrates whose domain included the land of Israel (Esther 3:12-14; cf. Ezra 5:6-17; 6:1-13; 7:21-25; 8:36; Nehemiah 2:7-9; Ezekiel 38:2, 5).

Haman and his horde would have come down into Israel from the north since invasions into Israel and this general area came primarily from the northern part of the country (Jeremiah 1:13-16; 3:18; 4:6; 6:1, 22; 10:22; 13:20; 23:7; 25:9; 46:20, 26; Ezekiel 26:7; cf. Ezekiel 38:6, 15; 39:2). Haman's horde would have come against Israel using the weapons as it literally states in Ezekiel 38 and 39. Contemporary prophecy writers like Tim LaHaye have conceded that their claim to a literal interpretation presents problems on how to interpret the weapons used in the attack and their disposal by fire. John Walvoord mentioned this in his book *The Nations in Prophecy.* "There are some other problems in the passage which merit study. A reference is made to bows and arrows, to shields and chariots, and to swords. These, of course, are antiquated weapons from the standpoint of modern warfare." Noting the obvious he writes, "This certainly poses a problem."[6] The problem being, as Time LaHaye pointed out, is, "How do you burn steel?"[7] Zola Levitt and Thomas McCall noticed the same problem. "It would be fitting indeed for the Israelis to watch a seven-year memorial fire symbolizing still another defense of the promised land. But how can they burn tanks, trucks, and armored vehicles? How can weapons of modern conflict be destroyed by fire?"[8]

In order to get around the force of what Ezekiel is literally saying, contemporary prophecy writers have gone symbolic. They have argued on one hand that "The Russians have perfected an actual wooden rifle. They have compressed wood until it is harder than steel, but lighter to carry. It is still combustible."[9] This compressed wood is called Lignostone that Russia has supposedly been using for years in the manufacturing of their weapons platforms such as tanks and planes.[10] However, as Ron Rhodes, a contemporary prophecy writer that believes Ezekiel 38 and 39 is yet future noted in his book *Northern Storm Rising*, "The context of Ezekiel 38 and 39 gives no indication that we should interpret it symbolically."[11] Paul Lee Tan drives the point home when he writes:

"There are some prophecies which, in describing eschatological warfares, predict that the weapons to be used then will be bows and arrows, chariots and horses, spears and shields. Are these to be taken literally? If we adhere strictly to the proper view of prophetic form, we must consider these weapons the same as that which will be used in eschatology. They must not be equated with vastly different modern war devices, as the H-bomb or the supersonic jet fighter."[12]

The other argument put forward by contemporary prophecy writers is that warfare will revert back to using old fashioned weapons.[13] John Walvoord laid out a couple of scenarios that he believed would play out in a way that would cause militaries to revert to wooden weapons. One scenario that he laid out "is that the battle [of Gog and Magog] is preceded by a disarmament agreement between nations. If this were the case, it would be necessary to resort to primitive weapons easily and secretly made if a surprise attack were to be achieved. This would allow a literal interpretation."[14] Another scenario that Walvoord laid out was "based on the premise that modern missile warfare will have developed in tht day to the point where missiles will seek out any considerable amount of metal. Under these circumstances, it would be necessary to abandon the large use of metal weapons and substitute wood such as indicated in the primitive weapons."

Walvoord continues on, "Whatever the explanation, the most sensible interpretation is that the passage refers to actual weapons pressed into use because of the peculiar circumstances of that day."[15]

Gary DeMar has pointed out how these scenarios show "how getting away from what the Bible actually says leads to ridiculous interpretation."[16] It proves Tim LaHaye's point if an interpreter does not assign words written in the Bible its *normal* meaning that it would have in its *normal* usage, then "everything is up for grabs. You can invent any kind of "interpretation" you want."[17] To re-quote Paul Benware: "Whenever we come to a prophetic passage, our commitment must be to understand that passage according to the accepted laws of language and not to seek some mystical figurative interpretation."[18]

A better and more literal interpretation is that Haman and his confederates would have been riding horses and chariots (Ezekiel 38:4; 39:20) armed with bow, arrows, swords, shields, war clubs, spears, helmets, and bucklers (Ezekiel 38:4, 15; 39:3, 9) as the text literally states. The fact that these weapons are made from wood is proven by the returning Jewish exiles not needing to not take wood from the fields or cut it from the forests (Ezekiel 39:10).

There would have been such an over-abundance of wood from the fallen soldiers that it would have been unnecessary for the Jews to gather it from the field or to cut down trees. There would have been enough wood to last for seven years (Ezekiel 39:9).

Haman and his forces would have come against the Jewish exiles living in the unwalled land of Israel since it had been desolated at the hands of the Babylonians and whose peace was finally secured by King Darius. (II Kings 25:10; Esther 9:19; Jeremiah 7:34; 10:22; 12:11; 25:8-11; 33:10; Lamentations 2:8-9; 5:18; Ezekiel 6:14; 12:20; 15:8; 33:27-29; Micah 3:12; Zechariah 7:14; cf. Nehemiah 2:8, 11-17; 4:1-10, 13-21; 6:1; Ezekiel 38:11). The plunder that Haman and his confederates would have wanted are the very items listed in Ezekiel 38:13 and would have come from the Israelites that were returning home from exile. The plunder would have been given to the soldiers as payment for those who participated in the invasion (Ezra 1:1, 4, 6; 6:5, 9; 7:15-20; cf. Esther 3:9, 11; 4:7; Ezekiel 38:13). "If God wanted to identify a future discovery of crude oil in Ezekiel 38 and 39, He could have chosen any of the Hebrew terms already in use at that time to make the point. If God could use arrows to symbolize missiles, as some futurists claim, then He could have added "pitch" to gold silver, cattle, and goods (Ezek. 38:13). These commodities, less the "pitch," are what the Jews brought back with them from their Bablyonian captivity (Ezra 1:4). This is another interpretive indicator that tells the reader that an ancient battle is in view."[19]

Once the full implication of Haman's plot had been understood by Ahasuerus (Esther 7:3-8), couriers were dispatched throughout the Persian Empire's 127 provinces, which would have included Israel, giving the Jews the ability to defend themselves from what would have been sure slaughter (Esther 8:5-14). "The king's edict granted the Jews in every city the right to assemble and protect themselves; to destroy, kill and annihilate any armed force of any nationality or province that might attack them and their women and children" (Esther 8:11). "A copy of the text of the edict was to be issued as law in every province and made known to the people of every nationality so that the Jews would be ready on that day to avenge themselves on their enemies" (Esther 8:13). It is more than conceivable that many of these invaders would have died "on the mountains of Israel (Ezekiel 39:4)" just as Ezekiel had prophesied since Haman's war against the Jews was to be waged throughout the Persian Empire including the land of Israel. Esther 9:16 says:

"Now the rest of the Jews who were in the king's provinces assembled, to defend their lives and rid themselves of their enemies, and kill 75,000 of those who hated them" (Esther 9:16).

The defeat of Haman's army in Esther 9:16 squares well with Ezekiel 39:2 where the majority of the invaders are destroyed. More were killed in the provinces than were actually killed in the city of Susa (500) with the majority being killed in the land of Israel (Esther 9:12-16). Again, it is more than conceivable that the slaughter was great enough that the invaders would have been "as food to all kinds of carrion birds and to the wild animals" and "For seven months the house of Israel will be burying them in order to cleanse the land" (Ezekiel 39:4; 39:12). Since Haman and his sons were descendants of Agag, an Amalekite the perpetual enemies of God, the deaths of Haman and his sons fulfill what the Lord said to Moses. "Write this on a scroll as something to be remembered and make sure that Joshua hears it, because I will completely blot out the memory of Amalek from under heaven"(Exodus 17:14, cf._Numbers 24:20; Deuteronomy 25:19). It is very plausible that while Haman was killed in Susa, he was buried on the mountains of Israel, along with his horde, to be seen as an example to those who would fight against God's people (Ezekiel 39:11). The why this is plausible has been pointed out by James Jordan. "According to Ezekiel 39:11 and 15, the place where the army of Gog is buried will be known as the Valley of Hamon-Gog, and according to verse 16, the nearby city will become known as Hamonah."[20] The Hebrew word for multitude found in Ezekiel 39:11, 15 and 16 is the word hamon "which is spelled in the Hebrew exactly like the name Haman... In Hebrew, both words have the same "trilateral root" (*hmn*). Only the vowels are different."[21] He goes on to state:

"Moreover, the words Agagite and Gog are the same in Hebrew, if we subtract the vowels and vowel-letters... Hamon-Gog and Haman the Agagite are identical. It seems to me that if I were a Jew living during the intertestamental era, I would be struck by these correspondences, and they would cause me to consider whether or not they are related."[22]

So how do we reconcile the Jews seizing the plunder in Ezekiel and yet not taking the plunder in Esther? Gary DeMar reconciles the two accounts this way:

"Ezekiel describes one aspect of what was done with the plunder. It was taken for a national cause, probably to assist in rebuilding the post-exile temple and the wall. Esther's account may indicate that the plunder was not to be taken and used by individuals: "they did not lay *their hands* on the plunder." The king granted the Jews as a *people*—as an exiled nation—the unconditional right "to plunder their spoil" (8:11). If Darius commanded that money from the "royal treasury out of taxes" (Ezra 6:8) be used to help to rebuild the temple, then it's conceivable that the plunder from Israel's enemies would also be used this way."[23]

This view by DeMar has a lot of validity to it. Consider this: since the weapons used in the invasion would have been made primarily from wood there would have been no reason for the Jews to go out and gather wood from the fields or the forest (Ezekiel 39:9-10). There would have been plenty of wood from the weapons taken from the dead invaders that it would last for seven years. The wood from the weapons could have been used in accordance with Leviticus 6:12-13:

"The fire on the altar must be kept burning; it must not go out. Every morning the priest is to add firewood and arrange the burnt offering on the fire and burn the fat of the fellowship offerings on it. The fire must be kept burning on the altar continuously; it must not go out."

The fact that the Jews played a part in defeating their enemies does not negate God's involvement in these events. Even though contemporary prophecy writers demand that God destroys the invaders supernaturally only, God has used supernatural events in the past to intimidate Israel's enemies that allowed and aided the Jews to physically rout their enemies (see Joshua 10:7-14). The fact that both Esther 9:5 and Ezekiel 38:21 mention swords as the weapons of choice should not be dismissed. God's intervention into this battle with supernatural events would have been enough to cause the necessary confusion that led to the infighting in Ezekiel 38:21 where "Every man's sword will be against his brother" while also allowing the Jews to defeat their enemies (see Joshua 10:7-14; Judges 7:21-22, I Samuel 14:20; cf. Esther 9:1-2, 5, 12, 16; Ezekiel 38:21).

The unexpected and overwhelming success of the Jews caused fear and dread to come over their enemies so much so that "No one could stand against them, because the people of all the other nationalities were afraid of them" (Esther 9:2).

"Many people of other nationalities became Jews because fear of the Jews had seized them" due to the overwhelming defeat of Haman by the Jews (Esther 8:17). This parallels and squares well with Ezekiel 39:21: "I will display my glory among the nations, and all the nations will see the punishment I inflict and the hand I lay upon them." Ezekiel 39:22 goes on to state, "From that day forward the house of Israel will know that I am the LORD their God." How does this not match up well with the events of Esther 9? The defeat of Haman was a great time of celebration for the Jews (8:16-17; 9:19) so much so that the Feast of Purim was instituted to remember their deliverance by God from Haman's evil scheme (Esther 9:23-32). The Feast of Purim was to be celebrated and observed without fail in every generation by every family (Esther 9:27-28). The Feast of Purim fulfills what Ezekiel prophesied: "From that day forward the house of Israel will know that I am the LORD their God" (Ezekiel 39:22).

Armageddon Now!

Contemporary prophecy writers like John Hagee and Tim LaHaye are very influential men within the Christian community especially here in America. Through organizations like Christians United for Israel, they have also been able to gain significant political clout and influence as well. "This melding of realpolitik and religion, say former and current U.S. officials, has produced a potent force. Israel's evangelical supporters "were out there before, but didn't really appear on the radar screen," says Dennis Ross, a Middle East envoy in the administrations of both George H.W. Bush and Bill Clinton. "Now they are an important part of the landscape.""[24]

Nevertheless, their political influence has put us on a high speed collision course with Armageddon. Through their political influence they have been able to marry their eschatology with foreign policy and it has people concerned:

> "[John Hagee] argues that the United States must join Israel in a pre-emptive military strike against Iran to fulfill God's plan for both Israel and the West. Shortly after the release of his book last January [2005], he launched Christian United for Israel (CUFI), a lobbying organization intended, as he says, to be a Christian version of the powerful American Israel Public Affairs Committee. With CUFI, which Hagee has said will cause a political earthquake, the televangelist

aims to put the political organizing muscle of the conservative evangelical movement behind his grand plan for a biblically prophesied end-time confrontation with Iran, which
will lead to the Rapture, Tribulation, and Second Coming of
Christ."[25]

The concern, and rightly so based on Hagee's comments, is
not only does Hagee want "God's plan – as he sees it – to
unfold, but to take an active role in seeing it happen."[26] As
Timothy Weber has well said:

"[Dispensationalists once] sat high on the bleachers on
history's fifty-yard line, watching as various teams took
their positions on the playing field below and explaining to
everyone who would listen how the game was going to end.
For the first one hundred years of their movement, then, they
were observers, not shapers, of events. But all that changed
after Israel reclaimed its place in Palestine and expanded its
borders. For the first time, dispensationalists believed that it
was necessary to leave the bleachers and get onto the playing
field to make sure the game ended according to the divine
script."[27]

People that are concerned about evangelical involvement into foreign policy see the involvement into American foreign affairs by evangelicals for exactly what it is. "Rabbi Jonathan Biatch of Temple Beth El in Madison, Wis. says. "The real bottom line is the fact that [Christian United for Israel] would like to exacerbate tensions in the Middle East so it will lead to Armageddon.""[28]

According to research done by The Barna Group pastor John Hagee is ranked as one of the top ten influential spokesmen among Pentecostals. "With that kind of influence, war with Iran or any other anti-Jewish nation might come about because this large end-time-driven voting-block could put pressure on politicians to vote in terms of eschatology."[29] With statements like "I would hope the United States would join Israel in a military pre-emptive strike to take out the nuclear capability of Iran for the salvation of Western civilization" because "The end of the world as we know it is rapidly approaching...rejoice and be exceedingly glad, the best is yet to be"[30] it is very difficult to dismiss such concerns.

The prophetic inevitability that is espoused by contemporary prophecy teachers is extremely dangerous.[31] It has lead to a "world-be-damned biblical hermeneutic that leads to an "alarmist" worldview [which] means that every negative newspaper headline is another support beam in an inevitable end-time constructed theology."[32] Therefore, "A world always on the precipice of some great and inevitable apocalyptic event is not in need of redemption but only of escape...Any attempt at reformation would be futile and contrary to God's unavoidable and predestined plan for Armageddon."[33] This world-be-damned attitude has led to an apathetic approach towards engaging society. "Rather than setting the standards for society, transforming lives, and creating culture, Christians have forgotten their call to be salt and light. We've allowed atheists and humanists to take control of education, government, arts, and sciences. Unlike our forefathers, we no longer have a vision for taking every thought captive to the obedience of Christ and taking dominion of every sphere of life for His Glory.

Marginalized as a "sub culture," many Christians are convinced that our social ills are signs that the end is near and that there is little that can be done. While waiting to be "Raptured" at any moment from the problems of the world, we are content to practice a juvenile and effeminate faith. Talking vegetables that represent Bible characters, irreverent T-shirts, music with shallow lyrics, self-help books, etc.

abound in Christian bookstores. These trivial things offer nothing to a world that desperately needs the transformational power of the Gospel."[34]

Gary DeMar has been one of the foremost leading critics of modern day prophetic writing and thought. In his hard hitting criticism of the kind of contemporary prophetic writing as espoused by Mark Hitchcock, Tim LaHaye, Hal Lindsey, and Thomas Ice, DeMar has pointed out that, "Bible prophecy, as it is practiced by today's mega-bestseller authors, is an *ex post facto* pseudo-science. The Bible's prophetic passages are retooled after reading the day's newspaper headlines."[35] Brandon Vallorani, picking up on DeMar's theme, stated, "Instead of taking scripture at face value, they use newspaper headlines as a filter to create complicated charts, introduce gaps between verses that go on for thousands of years (so far), and....have taken away our hope and vision for the future."[36]

David Chilton, who was considered by some to be the leading Bible scholar of our modern era before his passing, has comments on biblical interpretation that all interpreters should take to heart when interpreting the Bible:

"One of the most basic principles for an accurate under-standing of the Bible's message is that *Scripture interprets Scripture*. The Bible is God's holy, infallible, inerrant Word. It is our highest authority. This means we cannot seek for an authoritative interpretation of Scripture's meaning anywhere outside of the Bible itself. It also means that we must not interpret the Bible as if it dropped out of the sky in the twentieth century...This is the method we must use in solving every problem of interpretation in the Bible – including the prophetic passages. That is to say, when we read a chapter in Ezekiel, our first reaction must not be to scan the pages of the *New York Times* in a frantic search for clues to its meaning. The newspaper does not interpret Scripture, in any primary sense. The newspaper should not decide for us *when* certain prophetic events are to be fulfilled. Scripture inter-prets Scripture. This is the method we must use in solving every problem of interpretation in the Bible-including the prophetic passages."[37]

If we do not keep prophetic passages within their historical context, the danger of prophetic inevitability could eventu-ally become a nightmarish reality. Paul Boyer warned of this in 2003 as the war between the U.S. and Iraq was about to get under way. "As the nation debates a march toward war in the Middle East, all of us would do well to pay attention to the beliefs of the vast company of Americans who read the headlines and watch the news through a filter of prophetic belief."[38] If we continue to allow contemporary prophecy writers like John Hagee, Hal Lindsey, Mark Hitchcock, Thomas Ice, and Tim LaHaye to dictate how Bible prophecy should be interpreted, the Armageddon scenario that they continue to lay out in their books will become a self-fulfilling prophecy. They are rushing us ahead toward Armageddon!

Notes

[1] William MacDonald, "Ezekiel," *Believer's Commentary*, (Nashville, TN: Thomas Nelson, 1995) p.1036

[2] *Zondervan NIV Study Bible*, "Ezekiel," ed. Kenneth L. Barker (Grand Rapids, MI: Zondervan, 2002), p.1272, 1286. Compare this with Ezekiel 33:21-27 where a man that had escaped from Jerusalem told Ezekiel that the city had fallen. This message would have reached Ezekiel five months after the destruction of Jerusalem.Hal Lindsey has maintained that Ezekiel was written after the Babylonian Empire fell to the Medes and Persians in 539 B.C. In separate WorldNetDaily articles, he has given two dates for the book of Ezekiel. In his article *'Behold, I am against thee, O Gog'* Lindsey states that Ezekiel 38 and 39 was penned in 536 B.C. while in another article entitled *Iran, Russia and Ezekiel* he states that Ezekiel 38 and 39 was written circa 537 B.C. See Hal Lindsey, "'Behold, I am against thee, O Gog'", *WorldNetDaily* (December 15, 2006): http://www.worldnetdaily.com/news/printer-friendly.asp?ARTICLE_ID=53376; Hal Lindsey, "Iran, Russia and Ezekiel", (February 13, 2006): http://www.hallindseyoracle.com/articles.asp?ArticleID=12473.

[3] Kenneth Gentry, *Before Jerusalem Fell: Dating the Book of Revelation* (Powder Springs, GA: American Vision, 1998), p.17

[4] George Knight and James Edwards, *Compact Bible Handbook*, (Nashville, TN: Thomas Nelson Publisher Inc., 2004) n.p.

[5] Gary DeMar, Why the End of the World is Not in Your Future: Identifying the Gog-Magog Alliance (Powder Springs, GA: American Vision Press, 2008), p.39

[6] John F. Walvoord, *The Nations in Prophecy* (Grand Rapids, MI: Zondervan, 1967), p.115

[7] Tim LaHaye and Jerry Jenkins, Are We Living in the End Times?: Current Events Foretold In Scripture...and What They Mean (Carol Stream, IL: Tyndale House, 1999), p.89

[8] Thomas McCall and Zola Levitt, *The Coming Invasion of Israel* (Chicago, IL: Moody Press, 1974), p.44

[9] ibid, p.44

[10] Tim LaHaye, *The Beginning of the End* (Wheaton, IL: Tyndale House, 1972), p.80. Also see Tim LaHaye and Jerry Jenkins, *Are We Living in the End Times?: Current Events Foretold In Scripture...and What They Mean* (Carol Stream, IL: Tyndale House, 1999), p.89

[11] Ron Rhodes, Northern Storm Rising: Russia, Iran, and the Emerging End-Times Military Coalition Against Israel (Eugene, OR: Harvest House, 2008), p.95

[12] Paul Lee Tan, *The Interpretation of Prophecy* (Rockville, MD: Assurance Publishers, 1974), p.223

[13] Thomas McCall and Zola Levitt, *The Coming Invasion of Israel*, p.45

[14] John F. Walvoord, *The Nations in Prophecy*, p.116

[15] ibid, 116

[16] Gary DeMar, Why the End of the World is Not in Your Future, p.121

[17] Tim LaHaye, "Introduction", *The Truth Behind Left Behind: A Biblical View of the End Times* (Sisters OR: Multnomah Publishers, 2004), p.7

[18] Paul N. Benware, Understanding End Times Prophecy, p.24

[19] Gary DeMar, "The Danger of Prophetic Inevitability" (August 26, 2008): http://www.americanvision.org/article/the-danger-of-prophetic-inevitability/

[20] James B. Jordan, *Esther in the Midst of Covenant History* (Nicevelle, FL: Biblical Horizons, 1995), p.7

[21] ibid, p.7

[22] ibid, p.7

[23] Gary DeMar, Why the End of the World is Not in Your Future, p.62

[24] Andrew Higgins, "A Texas Preacher Leads Campaign To Let Israel Fight," *The Wall Street Journal* (July 27, 2006), p.A1

[25] Sarah Posner, "Pastor Strangelove," *The American Prospect* (June 6, 2006): http://www.prospect.org/web/page.ww?section=root&name=ViewPrint&articleId=11541

[26] Dave Eberhart, "Pastor John Hagee's D.C. Meeting Worries Jews," *NewsMax* (May 17, 2007): http://archive.newsmax.com/archives/articles/2007/5/16/211015.shtml

[27] Timothy P. Weber, On the Road to Armageddon: How Evangelicals Became Israel's Best Friend (Grand Rapids, MI: Baker, 2004), p .15; Qutoed in Hank Hanegraaff, The Apocalypse Code: Find Out What the Bible Really Says About the End Times...and Why it Matters (Nashville TN: Thomas Nelson, 2007), p.47-48

[28] Dave Eberhart, "Pastor John Hagee's D.C. Meeting Worries Jews,"

[29] Gary DeMar, "The Danger of Prophetic Inevitability" (November 12, 2007): http://www.americanvision.org/article archive2007/11-12-07.asp

[30] James D. Besser, "Hardline Pastor Gets Prime AIPAC Spot," *The Jewish Week* (March 9, 2007): http://www.thejewish-week.com/news/newscontent.php3?artid=13765&print=yes

[31] This issue was taken up by Dr. Dwight Wilson in his book *Armageddon Now!* where the dangers of prophetic inevitability led to a hands off approach by Christians with a premillennial view of Bible prophecy during the Holocaust. This hands off approach helped contributed to the deaths of six million Jews. The Holocaust was seen by premillennial Christians as a fulfillment of Bible prophecy where two thirds of the Jews are to perish during the Great Tribulation. This purge is supposed to cause the Jews to accept Jesus as the long awaited Messiah. Dwight Wilson, *Armageddon Now!: The Premillenarian Response to Russia and Israel Since 1917* (Tyler, TX: Institute for Christian Economics, [1977] 1991), p.94-97

[32] Gary DeMar, Why the End of the World is Not in Your Future, p.30

[33] ibid, p.31

[34] http://www.americanvision.org/article/mandate-28

[35] Gary DeMar, *Islam and Russia in Prophecy* (Powder Springs, GA: American Vision Press, 2005), p.13

[36] Brandon Vallorani, "Blessed Hope or False Hope?", *Biblical Worldview Magazine* (September 2006), p.13

[37] David Chilton, *The Great Tribulation* (Fort Worth, TX: Institute for Christian Economics, [1987] 1997), p.1-2

[38] Paul S. Boyer, "When U.S. Foreign Policy Meets Biblical Prophecy," *Alternet* (February 20, 2003): http://www.alternet.org/story/15221?page=entire

Appendix A

Nothing More Than Newspaper Exegesis

—◊—

"More than 2,500 years ago, a captive of the Babylonian Empire named Ezekiel penned a prophecy, dated for some future era called "the latter days," saying an alliance will arise, which Ezekiel calls collectively, "Gog, the land of Magog, the ruler of Rosh, Meschech and Tubal." It, together with an alliance led by Persia, including Turkey, makes up much of the Baltic region and the Mediterranean Middle East. Without taking up too much time, "Gog" refers to modern Russia, from Moscow (Meshech) to Siberia (Tubal). "Magog" refers to the states along the Black Sea, and in particular, the Republic of Georgia." [1]

This is how Hal Lindsey opens his WorldNetDaily article titled "Oh, my Gog!" in August 2008 right after the Russians invaded the tiny nation of Georgia a former satellite republic of the old Soviet Union. He went on to say, "Two thousand, five hundred years ago, a Hebrew captive living in Babylon outlined in detail the scenario that has continued to unfold and take shape in precise detail for most of the past generation."[2] In the article, he claimed that he outlined this scenario of Ezekiel's prophecy "in 1969 in my book "The Late, Great, Planet Earth" at a time most of this territory was a well-entrenched part of the Soviet Union."[3] He claimed that the invasion of Georgia by Russia is a sign that Russia wants to reclaim the territories of the old Soviet Empire in order to restore it to its former glory. Take special care to note what Hal Lindsey said. He stated that Ezekiel "*outlined in detail*" the events of chapters 38 and 39 going so far as to say that they have been outlined "*in precise detail.*" If that is indeed the case, then why have Lindsey and others changed the outline of Ezekiel 38 and 39 if what Ezekiel has said has been *outlined in precise detail.*

The problem is Lindsey outlined no such thing in his book *The Late Great Planet Earth.*

What he outlined in *The Late Great Planet Earth* is drastically different from what he wrote in his WorldNetDaily article. In his book *The Late Great Planet Earth,* as a part of his prophetic outline, he had the former communist nations of Poland, East Germany, and Czechoslovakia participating in the invasion of Israel.[4] In his August 2008 WorldNetDaily article, Lindsey never deals with how Poland, East Germany, and Czechoslovakia fit into the prophetic outline of Russia wanting to re-conquer and restore the former Soviet Empire. During the Cold War these nations where under the heavy influence of the Soviet Union. They were signatories of the Warsaw Pact which was the military treaty equivalent and counterpart to NATO. The Warsaw Pact, like that of NATO, was a pact between member nations that was created in the event that should any country in the pact were to be attacked the other countries in the pact would come to the defense of the attacked nation.

Of course, he couldn't deal with how these nations fit into his prophetic outline because the geo-political landscape has changed so drastically since *The Late Great Planet Earth* was published. When communism and the Berlin Wall fell, Poland became a staunch ally of the United States and was granted NATO membership in 1999 and membership into the

European Union in 2004. East Germany was reunified with West Germany to become a unified nation once again and the nations that once made up Czechoslovakia seceded from one another and Czechoslovakia is now called the Czech Republic and is also a member of the European Union.

In *The Late Great Planet Earth*, Lindsey predicted that Russia and Iran would be allies[5] yet when Russia invaded Afghanistan in 1979; he claimed that Russia would then invade Iran as prelude before marching on to Israel in its bid to control the Persian Gulf. "Before Russia attacks Israel, however, it will first invade Iran, or Persia, as it is called in Ezekiel chapter 38, verse five. When we apply this prophecy to modern times, it becomes obvious that the Soviets will use their recent conquest of Afghanistan as a springboard to overthrow Iran and gain control of the Persian Gulf area."[6]

But once communism was defeated, contemporary prophecy writers had to retool their books and come up with a new prophetic outline. Hal Lindsey even stated, "The collapse of the Soviet state was absolutely necessary to the fulfillment of biblical prophecy"[7] yet he never mentioned this in his previous books on prophecy. As a part of that new outline, Islam and countries that are Islamic such as Iran and Turkey have become the new antagonist pulling along an unwilling Russia. "The Bible says that a day is coming when the Islamic world will once again invade the nation of Israel but this time on an even larger scale and under the leadership of Russia."[8] Modern prophecy writers are now maintaining that Iran will be dragging an *unwilling* Russia in its failed invasion attempt against Israel.[9] I hope that you are seeing a consistent pattern here.

What contemporary prophecy writers are doing is nothing more than "newspaper exegesis." This kind of biblical interpretation is best defined as "simply studying current events rather than the Bible for clues to the future."[10] A good example of this kind of methodology can be found in Mark Hitchcock's book *The Coming Islamic Invasion* of Israel where he states that "Ezekiel is God's war correspondent for today's newspapers. We have gone through his inspired prophecy in Ezekiel 38-39 with our Bibles in one hand and today's newspaper in the other."[11] He goes on to further state, "we should study with our Bible in one hand and the newspaper in the other."[12]

Contemporary prophecy writers profile the newspaper headlines in order to make them fit an already preexisting view of prophecy. When a previous prediction of theirs becomes outdated due to the changing headlines, contemporary prophecy writers simply update what they had previously written in order for the prophecies of the Bible to be in line with the ever-changing winds that is geo-politics. Needless to say, the readers of their books are beginning to notice. The following are reviews on Mark Hitchcock's latest works on prophecy *Cashless: Bible Prophecy, Economic Chaos, and the Future Financial Order*[13] and *The Late Great United States: What Bible Prophecy Reveals about America's Last Days*[14] respectively:

> "This book was a disappointment. I expected it to have new information into current bible prophecy but it's just a re hash of information that's already out there. I could get the same information by watching Fox News. It also promotes the Pre Trib rapture very heavily. If you are pre trib and a novice to bible prophecy this book might be for you but if you are well versed in bible prophecy and/or not of pre trib rapture persuasion I would not buy this one." [15]

> "Unfortunately, as with any book of this type that deals with current events, much of the information is dated even though the book is relatively new. It was written before the Obama

administration took office, so his chapters on America being blessed because of their support for Israel is a little out of date since we are no longer the staunch allies of Israel we've always been since their inception. Since we are now trying to "reach out" to the "extremists" and told Israel they WILL be dividing Jerusalem, it will be interesting to see how America turns out from here. I took one star off because some of this seems a lot like filler. It's almost as if this was a booklet that was turned into a book." [16]

The methodology of "newspaper exegesis" is the worst way to interpret the Bible. "The newspaper has no prerogative to challenge God's word of truth. Nor do those who read the newspapers."[17] As Dr Andrew Corbett, a lecturer in hermeneutics at Tabor College has commented, "We should begin to interpret Bible Prophecy with the same basic principles of Biblical interpretation that we interpret any other passage of Scripture. Perhaps the first thing we should realize is that the Bible (including, and perhaps, especially, Bible Prophecy) was not written *to us* but it was written *for us*." [18]

Notes

[1] Hal Lindsey, "Oh, My Gog!" *WorldNetDaily.com* (August 22, 2008): http://www.worldnetdaily.com/index.php?pageId= 73063

[2] ibid

[3] ibid

[4] Hal Lindsey, *The Late Great Planet Earth*, (Grand Rapids, MI: Zondervan, 1970), p.69

[5] ibid, 67

[6] Hal Lindsey, *The 1980's: Countdown to Armageddon*, (New York, NY: Bantam Books, 1980), p.69

[7] Hal Lindsey, *Planet Earth–2000A.D.: Will Mankind Survive?* (Palos Verdes, CA: Western Front, 1994), p.197

[8] Mark Hitchcock, After the Empire: Bible Prophecy in Light of the Fall of the Soviet Union (Wheaton, IL: Tyndale House, 1994), p.109

[9] Hal Lindsey, "Iran, Russia and Ezekiel", (February 13, 2006): http://www.hallindseyoracle.com/articles.asp?ArticleID= 12473

[10] W. A. Young, Jr., What on Earth Is the Kingdom of God?: Understanding the Mystery of the Kingdom of God, (Fairfax, VA: Xulon Press, 2002), p.114

[11] Mark Hitchcock, *The Coming Islamic Invasion of Israel* (Sisters, OR: Multnomah, 2002), p.93

[12] Mark Hitchcock, *Iran: The Coming Crisis,* (Sisters, OR: Multnomah Press, 2006), p.189

[13] Mark Hitchcock, *Cashless: Bible Prophecy, Economic Chaos, and the Future Financial Order* (Eugene, OR: Harvest House, 2009)

[14] Mark Hitchcock, *The Late Great United States: What Bible Prophecy Reveals about America's Last Days* (Sisters, OR: Multnomah, 2009)

[15] http://tinyurl.com/yzjbtaa

[16] http://tinyurl.com/ylluo3u

[17] Greg L. Bahnsen, "The *Prima Facie* Acceptability of Postmillennialism," *Journal of Christian Reconstruction: Symposium on the Millennium,* ed. Gary North (Winter 1976), p.53

[18] Dr. Andrew Corbett, "Is the Bible Tomorrow's Newspaper?" (April 7, 2009): http://www.andrewcorbett.net/articles/2morrow/index.html

Appendix B

Dispensational Issues with Anti-Semitism

—〰—

During the presidential campaign of 2008, John Hagee caused a firestorm for the John McCain campaign over comments he gave in a sermon regarding Hitler which ultimately forced John McCain to have to reject Hagee's endorsement. What caused the firestorm was Hagee's assertion that Hitler and the Nazi persecution of the Jews were fulfilling God's will to restore the Jews back to the Promised Land in accordance with biblical prophecy. The comments in question came from a sermon that Hagee gave in the 1990's where he stated that God had used Adolf Hitler and the Nazi's to influence the desire of the Jews to return to Israel thus fulfilling Bible prophecy. According to media reports, Hagee had said the following:

> "God says in Jeremiah 16: 'Behold, I will bring them the Jewish people again unto their land that I gave o their fathers...Behold, I will send for many fishers, and after will I send for many hunters. And they the hunters shall hunt for them.' That would be the Jews...Then God sent a hunter. A hunter is someone who comes with a gun and he forces you. Hitler was a hunter."[1]

After this information was released and became headline news, Hagee released a statement claiming that his words had been taken out of context. "The intentional mischaracterization of my statements by an internet journalist seeking to use me as a political football in the upcoming presidential race is a gross example of bias at its worst. I will not stand idly by while my character is assassinated and my views on the Holocaust are grossly distorted. To assert that I in any way condone the Holocaust or that monster Adolf Hitler is the biggest and ugliest of lies. I have always condemned the horrors of the Holocaust in the strongest of terms."[2]

The problem for John Hagee is that these comments *were not* taken out of context. He said the same exact thing in his bestseller *Jerusalem Countdown: A Warning to the World*. In chapter nine, titled "The Second Exodus Begins," he echoed the very same sentiments from his earlier sermon regarding the Jewish return to Israel.[3] Hagee's comments were deemed anti-Semitic and with good reason. While Hagee's comments were certainly outrageous they are driven by his dispensational futuristic view of eschatology which sees the promises to Israel still unfulfilled (see chapter 5).

What's ironic is that Ed Hindson, in a National Liberty Journal article, claims that those who hold a preterist view as opposed to a futuristic view of eschatology are more inclined to lean toward anti-Semitism than a dispensationalist which is Hindson's and John Hagee's view. Quoting from his article *The New Last Days Scoffers* Hindson says, "While most preterists would insist they are not anti-Semitic, their theology certainly leans in that direction. One of the symbols of the current preterist movement is an artist's rendering of the smoldering ashes of Jerusalem in AD 70, as though they are rejoicing in the destruction of the Holy City."[4] He also calls preterism a "bizarre interpretation" and adds insult to injury by calling preterists last days scoffers. Hagee has ratcheted up the rhetoric, and for that matter hubris, by taking it a step further and insisting that those who do not subscribe to his view of eschatology are "carrying Hitler's anointing and his message"[5] and that message is the message of anti-Semitism!" which he calls "an ancient Godless heresy that is again raging through the Church masquerading as truth."[6] This is quite a charge considering that his system of eschatology has had problems with anti-Semitism in the not so distant past.

In his book *Armageddon Now!*, fellow premillennialist Dr. Dwight Wilson states how poorly dispensationalists handled anti-Semitism during World War II. He showed how people who believed as Hagee does, during World War II, were apathetic towards the Jewish persecution by the Nazi's since "persecution was prophetically expected, because it would encourage immigration to Palestine, because it seemed the beginning of the Great Tribulation, and because it was a wonderful sign of the [rapture]."[7] Not only were premillennialists apathetic towards the Jewish persecution at the hands of Hitler and the Nazi's, they were also ambivalent because it was seen as sign leading to the Great Tribulation and Israel's purification:

"Premillennialists were anticipating the Great Tribulation, "the time of Jacob's trouble." Therefore, they predicted, "The next scene in Israel's history may be summed up in three words: purification through tribulation." It was clear that although this purification was part of the curse, God did not intend that Christians should participate in it. Clear, also, was the implication that He did intend for the Germans to participate in it (in spite of the fact that it would bring them punishment)—and that any moral outcry against Germany would have been in opposition to God's will. In such a fatalistic system, to oppose Hitler was to oppose God."[8]

This ambivalence led to a hands off approach by premillenialists when it came to giving any kind of assistance to the Jews in Nazi Germany during World War II:

"Pleas from Europe for assistance for Jewish refugees fell on deaf ears, and "Hands Off" meant no helping hand. So in spite of being theologically more pro-Jewish than any other Christian group, the premillenarians also were apathetic— because of a residual anti-Semitism..."[9]

Jewish persecution prior to the Second Coming plays a big part in eschatological view of Hagee and those that share his view of the end-times. The prophetic view of Hagee and Hindson dictates that two-thirds of the Jews die in a Holocaust that would at least rival Hitler's. This is the assertion of John Walvoord. In his book *Israel in Prophecy* he stated:

"The purge of Israel in their time of trouble is described by Zechariah in these words: "And it shall come to pass, that in all the land, saith Jehovah, two parts therein shall be cut off and die; but the third shall be left therein. And I will bring the third part into the fire, and will refine them as silver is refined, and will try them as gold is tried" (Zechariah 13:8, 9). According to Zechariah's prophecy, two thirds of the children of Israel in the land will perish, but the one third that are left will be refined and be awaiting the deliverance of God at the second coming of Christ which is described in the next chapter of Zechariah."[10]

The sentiment expressed by Walvoord in 1962 was no different during World War II as premillennialists thought the massacre of Jews by the Nazi's would speed up the rapture, also called the blessed hope, of the church. "For the premillenarian, the massacre of Jewry expedited this blessed hope. Certainly he did not rejoice over the Nazi holocaust, he just fatalistically observed it as a "sign of the times.""[11] Therefore, "German anti-Semitism was accordingly seen as a fulfillment of prophecy."[12] As Gary North so aptly pointed out, "This is the grim prophetic trade-off that fundamentalists rarely discuss publicly, but which is the central motivation in the movement's support for Israel." He went on to state, "If Israel were militarily removed from history prior to the Rapture, then the strongest case for Christians' imminent escape from death would have to be abandoned. This would mean the indefinite delay of the Rapture. The fundamentalist movement thrives on the doctrine of the imminent Rapture, not the indefinitely postponed Rapture."[13]

Preterists on the other hand, who tend to be postmillennial in their view of eschatology, envision a future for Israel that does not see two-thirds of the Jews killed during the Great Tribulation. Postmillennarians, like their premillennarian brethren, believe that there will be a conversion of the Jews to Christ just not at the instigation of another Jewish holocaust that would at least rival Hitler's pogrom. "The Puritan form of postmillennialism generally holds not only to a future glory for the church, but that the millennial era proper will not begin until the conversion of the Jews and will flower rather quickly thereafter, prevailing over the earth for a literal thousand years."[14] For example, Martin Bucer "believed on the basis of Romans11:11-32 that a large scale conversion of the Jewish nation to Christianity would occur in history following the successful reformation of the church and the entrance into it of "the fullness of the Gentiles." All this, he believed, must necessarily precede the bodily return of Christ."[15]

As you can see, it is quite disingenuous for folks like Hagee and Hindson to label those that do not subscribe to the same view of prophecy as they do as anti-Semites when they fail to mention their own view's past issues with anti-Semitism. To say that preterism leads to anti-Semitism is ridiculous. Folks like Hagee and Hindson seem to have this obtuse notion that if you don't believe in their prophetic model, then you are somehow an anti-Semite because you're not pro-Israel. A cogent argument could be made that a postmillennial view of eschatology is more pro-Israel than premillennialism since it does not subject the Jews to another Hitler style wholesale slaughter.

Questioning today's popular eschatological views does not make one anti-Israel. In fact, to apply the prophecies to first century Israel instead of the whole world at the end of time is not only more Israel-centric but also more Israel friendly because it places the judgment upon those who were most responsible for rejecting their Messiah as opposed to condemning modern-day Jews who were not directly responsible. Also, a first century judgment vindicates Jesus as the Messiah because it accurately fulfills His own prophecies.[16]

As you can clearly see, it is not preterism that has issues with anti-Semitism but vice versa. But more than that, a person's eschatology is not what makes a person an anti-Semite. For those that are anti-Semitic they are that way not because of a particular view of eschatology, but because they were already anti-Semitic in their heart (Matthew 12:34; 15:18-20).

Notes

[1] "McCain rejects minister's endorsement" (May 22, 2008): http://www.cnn.com/2008/POLITICS/05/22/mccain.hagee

[2] ibid

[3] John Hagee, *Jerusalem Countdown: A Warning to the World,* (Lake Mary, FL: Frontline 2006), p.97

[4] www.nljonline.com/index.php?option=com_content& task=view&id=33&Itemid=37

[5] John Hagee, *Should Christians Support Israel?,* (San Antonio, TX: Dominion Publishers, 1987), p.132

[6] ibid, 1

[7] Dwight Wilson, *Armageddon Now!: The Premillenarian Response to Russia and Israel Since 1917* (Tyler, TX: Institute for Christian Economics, [1977] 1991), p.97

[8] Dwight Wilson, *Armageddon Now!,* p.94

[9] Dwight Wilson, *Armageddon Now!,* p.96-97

[10] John F. Walvoord, *Israel in Prophecy* (Grand Rapids, MI: Zondervan, 1962), p.108

[11] Dwight Wilson, *Armageddon Now!,* p.95

[12] Dwight Wilson, *Armageddon Now!,* p.94

[13] Gary North, "The Unannounced Reason Behind American Fundamentalism's Support for the State of Israel" (July 19, 2000): http://www.lewrockwell.com/orig/north7.html

[14] Kenneth L. Gentry Jr., "Postmillenialism," *Three views on the Millennium and Beyond*, eds. Darrell L. Bock and Stanley N. Gundry (Grand Rapids, MI: Zondervan, 1999), p.18

[15] Richard F. Lovelace, *Dynamics of Spiritual Life: An Evangelical Theology of Renewal* (Downers Grove, IL: InterVarsity, 1979), p.407

[16] http://www.romans11.org/articles/israel_esch4.htm

Select Bibliography

—⁂—

Blenkinsopp, Joseph. *Ezekiel: Interpretation, a Bible Commentary for Teaching and Preaching. Louisville*, KY: John Knox Press, 1990

Block, Daniel I. *The Book of Ezekiel: chapters 25-48*. Grand Rapids, MI: Wm. B. Eerdmans, 1998

Boe, Sverre. Gog and Magog: Ezekiel 38-39 as pre-text for Revelation 19, 17-21 and 20, 7-10. Tubingen: Moher Siebeck, 2001

Fredenburg, Brandon. *The College Press NIV Commentary: Ezekiel.* Joplin, MO: College Press Publishing Company, 2002

DeMar, Gary. End *Times Fiction: A Biblical Consideration of the Left Behind Theology.* Nashville, TN: Thomas Nelson, 2001

DeMar, Gary. *Islam and Russia in Prophecy.* Powder Springs, GA: American Vision, 2005

DeMar, Gary. W*hy the End of the World is Not in Your Future: Identifying the Gog-Magog Alliance.* Powder Springs, GA: American Vision, 2008

DeMar, Gary. *Zechariah 12 and the "Esther Connection": The Prophetic Fulfillment of the Rescue of Israel*. Powder Springs, GA: American Vision Press, 2005

Gumerlock, Francis X. *The Day and the Hour: Christianity's Perennial Fascination with Predicting the End of the World*. Powder Springs, GA: American Vision, 2000

Jordan, James B. *Esther in the Midst of Covenant History*. Niceville FL: Biblical Horizons, 1995

Wilson, Dr. Dwight. *Armageddon Now! The Premillenarian Response to Russia and Israel Since 1917*. Tyler, TX: Institute for Christian Economics, [1977] 1991

Tanner, J. Paul "Rethinking Ezekiel's Invasion of Gog," *Journal of the Evangelical Theological Society* 1996

Yamauchi, Dr. Edwin. *Foes From the Northern Frontier: Invading Hordes from the Russian Steppes*. Eugene, OR: Wipf and Stock, [1982] 2003

Zaspel, Fred G. "The Nations of Ezekiel 38 – 39: Who Will Participate in the Battle?" 1985

Dailey, Timothy J. *The Gathering Storm*. Tarrytown, NY: Revell, 1992

Hagee, John. Jerusalem Countdown: A Warning to the World. Lake Mary, FL: Frontline 2006

Hitchcock, Mark. *After the Empire: Bible Prophecy in Light of the Fall of the Soviet Union*. Wheaton, IL: Tyndale House, 1994

Hitchcock, Mark. *Iran: The Coming Crisis.* Sisters, OR: Multnomah Press, 2006

Hitchcock, Mark. *The Coming Islamic Invasion of Israel.* Sisters, OR: Multnomah, 2002

Hitchcock, Mark and Ice, Thomas *The Truth Behind Left Behind: A Biblical View of the End Times.* Sisters, OR: Multnomah Press, 2004

Lahaye, Tim. *The Beginning Of The End.* Wheaton, IL: Tyndale House, 1972

Lahaye, Tim. *The Coming Peace in the Middle East.* Grand Rapids, MI: Zondervan, 1984

LaHaye, Tim and Jenkins, Jerry B. *Are We Living in the End Times?: Current Events Foretold In Scripture...And What They Mean.* Carol Stream, IL: Tyndale House, 1999

Lindsey, Hal. *Planet Earth–2000A.D.: Will Mankind Survive?* Palos Verdes, CA: Western Front, 1994

Lindsey, Hal. *The 1980's: Countdown to Armageddon.* New York, NY: Bantam Books, 1980

Lindsey, Hal. *The Late Great Planet Earth.* Grand Rapids, MI: Zondervan, 1970

McCall, Thomas and Levitt, Zola. *The Coming Invasion of Israel.* Chicago, IL: Moody Press, 1974

Missler, Chuck. *The Magog Invasion.* Palos Verdes, CA: Western Front, 1995

Rhodes, Ron. *Northern Storm Rising: Russia, Iran, and the Emerging End-Times Military Coalition against Israel.* Eugene, OR: Harvest House, 2008

Rosenberg, Joel. Epicenter: *Why the Current Rumblings in the Middle East Will Change your Future.* Carol Stream, IL: Tyndale House, 2006

Walvoord, John with Hitchcock, Mark. *Armageddon, Oil and Terror: What the Bible Says about the Future* 3rd rev. ed. Carol Stream, IL: Tyndale House, 2007